Can You Relate?

Real-World Advice for Teens on Guys, Girls, Growing Up, and Getting Along

by Annie Fox, M.Ed.*

*also known as Hey Terra! as featured at Talk City's The InSite

Edited by Elizabeth Verdick

free spirit
PUBLISHiNG®

Works
for kids®

Library of Congress Cataloging-in-Publication Data

Fox, Annie, 1950–
      Can you relate? : real-world advice for teens on guys, girls, growing up, and getting along / by Annie Fox ; edited by Elizabeth Verdick.
          p. cm.
    Includes bibliographical references and index.
    Summary: Answers letters received by Talk City's "The InSite" and provides advice about dealing with authority figures, handling problems with parents and siblings, making a relationship work, finding and keeping real friends, sex, and more topics important to teens.
    ISBN 1-57542-066-X (pbk.)
    1. Teenagers—United States—Miscellanea. 2. Interpersonal relationships—Miscellanea. 3. Dating (Social customs)—United States—Miscellanea. [1. Dating (Social customs) 2. Interpersonal relations. 3. Teenagers. 4. Adolescence.] I. Verdick, Elizabeth. II. Title.

HQ796.F747 2000
305.235—dc21

99-046837

At the time of this book's publication, all facts and figures cited are the most current available; all telephone numbers, addresses, and Web site URLs are accurate and active; all publications, organizations, Web sites, and other resources exist as described in this book; and all have been verified. The author and Free Spirit Publishing make no warranty or guarantee concerning the information and materials given out by organizations or content found at Web sites, and we are not responsible for any changes that occur after this book's publication. If you find an error or believe that a resource listed here is not as described, please contact Free Spirit Publishing. Parents, teachers, and other adults: We strongly urge you to monitor children's use of the Internet.

Cover and interior design by Percolator
Index compiled by Randl Ockey

10 9 8 7 6 5 4 3
Printed in the United States of America

Free Spirit Publishing Inc.
217 Fifth Avenue North, Suite 200
Minneapolis, MN 55401-1299
(612) 338-2068
help4kids@freespirit.com
www.freespirit.com

To David—my love, my partner, my best friend, my rock—
always in all ways. Thank you for our unlimited relationship
of twenty-five years. It nurtures me in everything I do.

ACKNOWLEDGMENTS

Many good-hearted people spent days reviewing early drafts of *Can You Relate?* and sharing their ideas and suggestions with me. Their insights helped shape a manuscript into what I hope is a useful, compassionate book filled with highly accessible information. For that I thank Cheryl Amon, Kasey Arnold-Ince, David Fox, Deborah Roberts, Geoffrey Wild, and Jenna Woodul. Likewise, I'm indebted to my dear friend Peg Shalen, MFCC, whose compassionate and insightful work with teens has made her an invaluable resource to our community.

I'd also like to thank Talk City for giving Terra an online home. Without the support of Peter Friedman and company, Terra would have remained just another idea inside my head. Of course, this book wouldn't exist without the thousands of teens online around the world who reached out to Terra and trusted her to help them sort out their confusion, worries, fears, and dreams. Nothing pleases me more than knowing I've helped them.

Thank you to my editor at Free Spirit Publishing, Elizabeth Verdick. Her knowing hand guided the structure of what could have been a very unwieldy project. I wish also to acknowledge my agent, Harvey Harrison, a man who knows how to recognize, encourage, and promote ideas that can change the world. I'm honored to have him represent me.

Finally, I'd like to proclaim my love and admiration for my daughter, Fayette, and my son, Ezra. It has always been a delight and a great source of pride for me to be their mother. There's no doubt in my mind that they've taught me more about being a teen than I ever learned from being one myself.

CONTENTS

Chapter 4: Sex, Unhealthy Romantic Relationships, and Good-byes

INTRODUCTION

When my oldest child became a senior in high school, I knew it wouldn't be long before she left for college. I felt happy that she was about to start a new chapter in her life and proud of her success in getting to this point. But I also felt sad. Not only was I going to miss having my smart, funny, talkative, wildly creative daughter living at home, but I was also going to miss her wonderful friends. I wouldn't hear what was going on in their day-to-day lives anymore, and I wouldn't be able to help them sort things out.

I began thinking about ways to continue helping teens after my daughter and her friends moved on. One morning, I woke up with an idea and shared it with my husband, who's Director of New Content for Talk City, a large network of online communities. I would create a special online teen "neighborhood" where young people could make the world (and their corners of it) a safer, saner, cleaner, more equitable place to live. Talk City's The InSite *(www.talk city.com/theinsite)* launched in June 1997.

At The InSite, you can find everything from advice on relationships, to a teen soap opera called *The Story*, to an online gallery for teen art and writing. At the heart and soul of The InSite is "Terra," a kind of cyberspace "Dear Abby" who answers thousands of letters (from Hong Kong to Brazil) written by teens just like you. Terra, the Latin word for Earth, is my online name.

About a dozen times a day, I receive email messages like this one:

Hey Terra,

My best friend has never had a girlfriend and I've had lots of them, but I'm always really nice to him about it, never bragging or anything like that. Anyway, two weeks ago I told him about this girl I REALLY like a lot and asked him what he thought of her. All he said was, "She's okay." But last weekend, we were all at this party and he was totally flirting with the girl I like! I got really mad and called him a backstabber and a couple of other names. He didn't talk to me for the rest of the party and ended up getting a ride home with someone else. When I called him the next day, he hung up on me. Now I hear he's going out with that girl! It looks like I lost the girl and my best friend. Help! What should I do?

Alone and Sad

When I read letters like this one, I'm reminded of how complicated it is to be a teen, especially when it comes to relationships. Sometimes you say stuff you don't mean to people you really care about, and they feel hurt and angry. And sometimes you can't, no matter how hard you try, say the things you really *do* mean. And then, because of what you *didn't* say, people feel hurt and angry. It's challenging to make relationships work when you haven't had much practice talking about your feelings—feelings that are often intense, mixed up, and constantly changing. This is why it's often difficult for others to understand what's going on with you and for you to understand yourself without help.

And this is where Terra comes in. I read every email addressed to Terra, and I personally answer each one. I'm here to help young people improve their relationships because I believe everyone (including you) deserves to be happy and treated with respect. My goal is to help you understand your feelings and to show you how to build healthier relationships with your friends, boyfriends/girlfriends, parents, siblings, teachers, coaches, and others.

This book includes more than one hundred letters from teens who wrote to me for advice. (To protect the teens' privacy, I decided not to use real names or any specific details that might identify a particular letter writer. Still, the letters and situations are absolutely real.) The letters let you find out what other teens are going through and see how their experiences are similar to your own.

As you read the letters, think about the questions and answers. Then ask yourself:

- How are these issues similar to mine?
- How are they different?
- If I were in these kinds of situations, what would I do?
- Do Terra's answers make sense to me?
- Could Terra's advice help me or a friend, now or in the future?

Maybe you're thinking, "What makes her such an expert on relationships?" I don't claim to be an expert (and neither does Terra!). But, just like you, I've had experiences that have taught me about myself and life. As a student, a teacher, a writer, a traveler, an actor, a director, a daughter, a sister, an aunt, a friend, a mom, and a wife, I've spent years becoming comfortable with who I am and learning what it takes to get along with others. My advice is always based on what I know about healthy relationships, which are the only kind worth having.

Being a teen is sometimes tough—no doubt about that. And relationship issues are part of the challenge. But these issues *can* be worked out. I believe that having successful relationships always comes down to this:

1. Be clear about who you are and what's important to you.
2. Be aware of your feelings.
3. Be honest and direct when you communicate.
4. Treat other people with sensitivity and respect.

While no relationship is "perfect," every one of yours can be healthy. And having healthy relationships is a good way to learn, have fun, and grow in positive ways. If you know what's right for you and how to express your feelings, you'll have better relationships—guaranteed.

Adolescence doesn't last forever. (For some of you out there, that's probably good news.) My daughter just finished her teen years, and my son just started his. Like them, you and all of your friends are on a journey. When you're lost and confused, sometimes you need someone who will listen and help you figure out your next step. If you need advice, please write to me. Mail letters to me in care of:

Free Spirit Publishing Inc.
217 Fifth Avenue North, Suite 200
Minneapolis, MN 55401-1299

Or email me at:
help4kids@freespirit.com

I look forward to hearing from you!

In friendship,
Annie Fox

CHAPTER 1

Me, Myself, and I

This book is about the relationships in your life and how to make and keep them healthy. But before you start thinking about how you relate to others, it makes sense first to understand your relationship with *yourself*. The way you feel about yourself affects nearly every choice you make. This includes your behavior, your attitude, and your goals, as well as the people you choose to hang out with and get close to.

So what kind of relationship do you have with yourself? How well do you even know yourself? What are your strengths? What are your weaknesses? Are you aware of your own feelings and how to express them in healthy ways? Are you comfortable in new situations? When dealing with people you don't agree with, do you stand up for yourself and your beliefs?

Not sure of all the answers yet? That's okay. Life's for learning, and learning about yourself is an excellent place to start. The better you know yourself and what's right for you, the easier it is to make wise choices. And wise choices are the ones that keep you moving in a positive direction.

WHAT'S UP WITH PEER PRESSURE?

As a teen, you deal with all kinds of peer pressure every day—even from people you consider friends. This probably isn't news to you, because you know that your peers (whether they're friends or not) heavily influence how you dress, act, feel about things, and deal with those feelings.

So what's it like when you're with your friends? Do you do things *their* way or your own? Which one's the "right" way? And how do you know?

If your way feels right and you go with that, you may worry about losing your friends. But doing what you believe in strengthens your self-respect. (And that counts for a lot!) On the flip side, if you ignore what feels right and do something so people will think you're "cool," you may feel as if you've betrayed yourself. And that's not a good feeling at all. Nearly everyone wants to be liked, but how much of yourself and what you believe in do you have to give up to be popular? Whenever you're faced with a heavy-duty decision or a simple choice, take a moment to ask yourself, "What should I do?" The answer will come from your *inner voice* (some people call it a *conscience*). This voice or gut feeling tells you, on a very personal level, what's right for you.

Maybe you didn't even know that you had an inner voice, so you're not exactly sure what it sounds like. To find out, imagine yourself in the following situation and pay attention to what you hear inside your head.

 You're grounded because you told your parents that you were at a friend's house, and they found out you were really at a party they had said you couldn't go to. Now it's Saturday night, and you're home alone. Your parents are out and won't be back until late. Your best friend calls and invites you to a movie that you both really want to see. Your friend knows you're grounded but guarantees you'll be back long before your parents return. Should you go to the movie or not?

In this situation, your friend is pressuring you to break your parents' rules (again!). Obviously, it would be fun to see the movie, but you could get caught—and you're already in trouble. Part of you is probably scared and doesn't want to risk it, but another part may feel angry that you were punished in the first place. On the one hand, it might be exciting to try to get away with breaking the rules again; but on the other hand, would you be able to enjoy the movie worrying about what would happen if your parents came home before you got back?

With so many conflicting feelings, it's a challenge to hear your inner voice. This is why it's important to quiet things down inside your head, so you can really listen to your inner voice's advice. Start thinking about the choices (going to the movie or staying home) and what you might gain and lose with each one.

Picture yourself going to the movie: How do you feel seeing your friend? Standing in line? Watching the movie? What's it like when you get home? Imagine that you return before your parents do. How do you feel? Imagine them coming into your room later to say good night. How do you feel then? Imagine that your parents arrive home early. How do they feel when they realize you're not there? What happens when you get home?

Now picture yourself saying no to the movie and staying home. What do you do to keep from being bored? How do you feel while you're doing it? How do you feel when you think about your friend at the movies with someone else? How do you feel when your parents get home?

Which choice creates more positive feelings? Which choice creates more negative ones? Which one feels "right"? When you hear the answer to that question inside your head, that's your inner voice talking to you. Listen to it. Trust it. Your inner voice will help you feel good about yourself and the decisions you make.

Kids bug me because I'm different

Hey Terra,

I've never been like anyone else I know. I'm not sure why, and I don't really care. My problem is I'm sick of people making all kinds of judgments about me just because I act different. How can I get the kids in my school to stop pressuring me and just leave me alone?

Boppin' Unique

Dear Boppin' Unique,

The best way to avoid the pressure and judgments is to keep listening to your inner voice. This voice is telling you that you don't need to be like everyone else.

Being unique can be lonely, so look around for allies. Who are the kids at your school who aren't afraid to be themselves? Which ones are most accepting of differences and would appreciate you for who you are? Reach out to them in friendship and forget about the rest. If there's no one like this at your school, look for friends elsewhere. Let your interests (sports, music, art, a hobby) guide your out-of-school activities. Get out there and find people you can relate to.

It might help to read the biographies of interesting people who found their unique paths in life. Remember, unique people are one of a kind because they dare to be different, and they help change the way all of us think about the world. If everybody looked and acted like the next person, life would be very dull. Stay true to yourself!

In friendship,
Terra

> **If I stand up for someone, other people might not like me anymore**

Send ▷

Hey Terra,

A guy I've known and liked from a distance is coming to my school! We both play clarinet in the orchestra, so I'm sure we'll get to know each other lots better. This is fine with me, except I just found out there's a group of kids in my school who know him and hate him. If I start being friendly toward him, they're probably going to hate me, too. Which is more important: to be friends with this guy or to make sure these other kids like me?

Friend

Dear Friend,

Chances are, there will always be people who disapprove of something about the way you live your life. Maybe it's the music you like, how you dress, the way you vote, or the people you choose as friends. As the saying goes, "You can't please all of the people all of the time." So you might as well please yourself and do what *you* know is right.

You expect your friends to stand up for you, in spite of what others say, right? That's just an unwritten rule of friendship. Try being that kind of friend to this guy. Maybe you can find out why the other kids dislike him. Their opinions might be based on assumptions and lies. If this guy knew what was being said about him behind his back, he could try to set the record straight or apologize. Either way, knowing what's going on could help him get along with people in his new school. Be a friend and do what you can to help! I wish you well.

In friendship,
Terra

Why should people care if the girl I like is only a sophomore?

Hey Terra,

There's a girl I would really like to go out with, and I think she likes me, too, but she's only a sophomore. I'm a senior and that could present some problems. I'm getting all kinds of opinions. What do you think I should do?

Older Guy

Dear Older Guy,

A senior going out with a sophomore seems fine to me. This isn't a significant age difference, though if you said you wanted to go out with a girl who's in seventh grade, I'd say no way!

Generally speaking, a two-year age difference between high-school students isn't a problem. However, some people in your school might give you a hard time. They may tease you about not being able to find a girlfriend your own age. They might even try to pressure you to forget the idea altogether.

But none of this has anything to do with your wanting to get to know this girl better. What matters is doing what's right for you. You don't need anyone else's approval. Follow your heart!

In friendship,
Terra

RIDING EMOTIONAL WAVES

Emotions (feelings) come and go like waves. Sometimes you feel intensely angry, sad, or scared. Other times, you feel intensely happy, embarrassed, or confused. This is true for everyone, but especially for teens, whose emotional swings can be frequent and dramatic.

What can you do about emotional waves? Learn to understand them. Emotions are triggered, in part, by hormones and events in your life. You don't necessarily choose your emotions, and you can't prevent them. Emotions happen; that's what makes us human.

It helps to understand that you and your emotions are separate. You *have* feelings (and they may be powerful), but your feelings aren't *you*. You are your thoughts, dreams, talents, skills, goals, memories, experiences, and *much* more.

So when emotional waves wash over you, make a conscious choice to express these feelings in healthy ways. You can talk to someone, write in a journal, or go for a walk or run. Once you're seeing things more clearly (instead of through waves of emotion), start working on what's bothering you and find a positive solution.

Here's another way of thinking about your emotions: you can't control the waves, but you can learn to ride them, stay afloat, and not get dragged down by the undertow. It isn't easy, but learning to identify, accept, and express your feelings in healthy ways is an important part of growing up.

Anger

The world presents plenty of things to get angry about: war, injustice, poverty, environmental abuse, and so on. But it doesn't do you (or the world) any good to direct your anger at other people or to turn it inward where it eats away at you. Instead, you can choose to deal with anger in *positive* ways. If, for example, you're outraged about an animal-rights issue, channel your anger into speaking out, organizing letter-writing campaigns, or volunteering at an animal shelter. This way, you're doing something productive with the extra energy that anger produces in your body.

Sometimes it's not a situation but a person who sparks your anger. Depending on your mood, it may not take much to make you mad. Suppose someone jokes about the way your hair looks today. While the person may not have meant anything by it, you might get angry or even feel as if your day is ruined. Something that wasn't supposed to be a big deal has just become one. Other times, the cause of your anger really *is* a big deal, like when a friend betrays your trust. You may feel so angry and hurt that you wonder if you'll ever get over it.

No matter what causes your anger, bottling it up inside won't help. You have to let it out. This is the best way to deal with it.

For many people, releasing anger means yelling, swearing, plotting revenge, or using physical violence. How do *you* handle anger? If you're upset with a friend, do you say mean things or bring up hurt feelings from the past? Maybe you stop talking to the person altogether, and the friendship ends. How about when you get mad at your brother or sister? Do you scream and threaten? Hit? Throw things? Do you storm into your room and slam the door, silently hating everyone and everything?

If any of this sounds familiar, you already know that dealing with anger in these ways doesn't feel good. But did you know that these behaviors aren't healthy? Acting out or holding in anger doesn't solve anything. In fact, it often makes the situation worse.

The good news is you can learn to express your anger without being violent or hurtful. Whenever you're mad at someone, take some time to calm down before you react. Then follow these steps to help yourself get a grip:

1. Get away from the person you're angry with. Before you and the other person can resolve the conflict, you have to gain control of yourself. Explain that you need some time alone, and then find a quiet place to think.

2. Take some slow, deep breaths. Deep breathing will slow down your racing heart and help you clear your mind. Count to twenty-five in your head—slowly. This is a chance for you to calm down and get some perspective on what happened.

3. Think about the situation. It takes at least two people to create a conflict. What was your part in this one? Ask yourself the following questions and think carefully about your answers: What did I do that added to the conflict? What did I forget to do that added to it? What do I wish I'd said or done instead of what I actually said or did? What could I do differently next time?

4. Look at the conflict from the other person's point of view. Imagine how he/she feels about what happened between you. If you were that person, how would *you* have acted or reacted?

5. Write down exactly what you'd like to say to this person. A journal is a good place for this type of writing. You don't have to show it to anyone, so don't hold back. Keep writing until you get a lot of the anger out of your system.

6. Read aloud whatever you wrote. (You're alone, so make the reading as dramatic as you want.) Do you feel better after getting out some of that anger? Is there any left? If so, write more things you'd like to say to the person. Then read the whole thing aloud again.

Once you feel calm, think about what you're actually going to say to the person. Of course, you may never want to talk to him/her again, but if the relationship is worth saving, you'll need to have an honest, heartfelt conversation.

Wondering what to say? Or how the other person will react to your words? In Chapter 9, "Conflict Resolution Tool Kit," you'll find advice about sharing your feelings and listening to others with openness and respect.

I get mad about everything

Hey Terra,

My problem is that I get so mad about EVERYTHING!!! My parents aren't all that strict, but whenever they tell me I can't do something, I feel like punching them out. I've never actually hit anyone, but I really feel like it a lot of the time. If my younger sister forgets to give me a phone message or something, I completely lose control and chew her out. Then she starts crying and I feel bad, but I don't know what to do. Sometimes I yell so much that my throat gets sore.

Also, my good buddy has started getting on my nerves. He doesn't have a girlfriend, and sometimes he says bad stuff about mine, like how he saw her flirting with this other guy. I got really mad at my girlfriend, but it turned out it wasn't even true that she was flirting, so she got mad at me, and we broke up even though I still like her. Then I got really mad at my friend for telling me a lie in the first place! Is there something I can do to not get so angry about everything?

MAD!!

Dear MAD,

It sounds like when you get angry, you stop thinking straight. Then you jump to conclusions and say things that hurt other people's feelings—which ends up hurting you, too.

Many people have trouble coping with their anger. It's good that you realize you have a problem dealing with anger and you want to change. This issue may be best handled with the help of an adult you trust. Is there a teacher or school counselor you can talk to? A youth group leader? A parent?

Help yourself by becoming more aware of the warning signs that you're about to explode. Your heart may start pounding. Blood may rush to your head. You may even get the feeling that you're "seeing red." When you experience these physical reactions, *remove yourself from the situation*. If you can't physically leave (because you're in a car or classroom), take slow, deep breaths until you calm down. Think "relax."

Once you're calm enough to talk without screaming, cursing, or saying something hurtful, let the person know how you feel about what happened. Then give him/her a chance to tell the other side of the story. Conflicts are a lot easier to resolve when people talk to each other with respect and a willingness to listen.

One last thing: Be patient with yourself. Don't expect to change overnight. It takes practice to learn how to handle anger in positive ways, but it's definitely worth the effort. You can do it!

In friendship,
Terra

Cage Your Rage for Teens: A Guide to Anger Control by Murray C. Cullen and Joan Wright (Lanham, MD: American Correctional Association, 1996). Using their years of experience dealing with prison inmates (a very angry population), the authors present a guide to anger management designed especially for teens.

Straight Talk About Anger by Christine Dentemaro and Rachel Kranz (New York: Facts On File, 1995). This book gives teens information and advice on what the authors call "the misunderstood emotion." You'll find tips on keeping an anger log, talking to other people, and coping with anger in healthy, productive ways.

Winning! How Teens (and Other Humans) Can Beat Anger and Depression by Lew Hamburger, Ph.D. (New York: Vantage Press, 1997). Written especially for teens, this practical, helpful book talks about the causes and treatments of anger and depression.

Talk City's The InSite
www.talkcity.com/theinsite/me/me_fires.html
This section of The InSite deals with overwhelming feelings like anger and aggression. "Been There" stories by teens who have struggled with anger, rage, and depression describe the valuable life lessons these young people learned during tough times.

Embarrassment

Have you ever wished you could vanish from the planet because of something you said or did? Everyone has embarrassed themselves at one time or another (yes, even the coolest people you know). No one's perfect, and we all make mistakes. It's called being human.

When you do something embarrassing, like knocking over a soda, missing a foul shot, or asking a question that the teacher says he *just* answered, give yourself a break. At these moments, it may feel as if *everyone* is staring at you, laughing, and thinking that you're a complete idiot. But this just isn't true! Most people are much too concerned about their own mistakes to focus on yours.

If you think you've made a fool of yourself and don't know what to do next, follow these tips on dealing with embarrassment:

1. Admit that you're feeling embarrassed. Don't get defensive or try to hide your feelings. You might even laugh and say, "Whoa! Am I embarrassed!" The feelings will pass more quickly if you don't try to cover them up or pretend they don't exist.

2. Forgive yourself. You made a mistake. It happens. Stop beating yourself up. If you've hurt or embarrassed someone else, apologize. Sometimes this is the hardest part, but it's important to say you're sorry, because it will make both you and the other person feel better.

3. Move on. Put the embarrassing moment where it belongs: *in the past.* Push yourself if you have to but get on with your life. If someone kids you about what happened, say, "Oh, yeah! That was pretty embarrassing." Laugh and show that you can handle the teasing. Other people will soon forget about the embarrassing moment—and you will, too.

4. Think before you act or speak. Remembering this will save you from some embarrassing moments. There's no guarantee that it will prevent *all* embarrassments, but it can help reduce them. And when you slip up, repeat tips 1–3 to recover more quickly.

I always make a fool of myself

Hey Terra,

No one knows this, but I'm really afraid of getting into situations that will embarrass me. It happens all the time, no matter how careful I am. It's gotten so bad lately that I don't even raise my hand in class because I'm afraid of saying something stupid. I don't want to hang out with other people because I just know I'm going to end up saying something embarrassing. You're probably thinking, "Like what?" I could give you a whole long list, but it's too embarrassing! I'm probably missing out on a lot of fun because of this. I need help!

Embarrassed Guy

Dear Embarrassed Guy,

What's your fear of embarrassment based on? What specific things have you done in the past that embarrassed you? Write down a few of these memories and recall what happened each time you messed up. How did other people react? After you felt embarrassed, what happened?

No matter how many embarrassing moments we have (and believe me, we all have them), we survive and life goes on. Even though people say, "I could have died of embarrassment," no one really dies from this feeling. Each time the fear of embarrassment stops you from doing something, repeat to yourself, "No one ever died of embarrassment, and neither will I."

If this doesn't help, talk to a school counselor or another trusted adult about your problem. It's important not to let fear stop you from socializing and having fun. And remember, one of the biggest mistakes a person can make is to always be afraid of making one! Good luck!

In friendship,
Terra

Insecurity

Have you ever felt as if you're really two people in one? Maybe one side of you is cool, outgoing, and funny. But these qualities are hidden by your shy, awkward, and not-so-cool side. Or maybe on the *outside* you're popular and social, but on the *inside*, you're unsure of yourself. Perhaps, like many people, you worry that you wouldn't be accepted if everybody knew the *real* you.

There are times when everyone—even famous athletes, actors, and pop stars—feels trapped in a prison of self-doubt. The prison walls can become so thick that it's nearly impossible to break out, try new things, and enjoy life.

When you're a teen, your interests, attitudes, and feelings about yourself change often—sometimes daily. With so much change, it can be difficult to feel confident, especially in new situations. People who are unsure of themselves and their ability to succeed can get stuck in an insecurity trap. If you're in this trap, you might hold yourself back and miss out on wonderful opportunities.

How can you escape from the trap? One of the best ways is to figure out what you're good at. By focusing on your strengths (talents, abilities, positive traits), you'll start feeling more secure about yourself. Here's how to begin:

1. Make a list of your strengths. You might include things like "People know they can count on me" or "I'm a good listener." Or you could list any special skills you have like telling jokes, drawing, singing, playing soccer, or being a good student.

2. Make a list of your weaknesses. What traits are preventing you from being happy or self-assured? We're not talking about looks! Focus on personality traits that need work or skills you might improve on. For example, "I put off things until the last minute" or "I don't always tell the truth about how I feel."

3. Keep both lists the same size. If you think of five weaknesses, come up with five strengths. If you have a hard time identifying your strengths, ask a parent or a friend for suggestions.

4. Review your strengths. How do you feel about them? Does the list include things you don't usually give yourself credit for? If so, give yourself credit now. And think about how you can use these strengths more than you already do. Write down your ideas, so you can turn them into goals.

5. Review your weaknesses. Identify the weaknesses you can live with for now and think about the ones you want to work on. Don't tackle everything at once. Instead, choose one weakness and develop a plan of action. For example, if you want to stop putting things off until the last minute, think of ways to get more organized about deadlines. Maybe you can break down a long-term assignment into several small steps. This way, you'll be more likely to make steady progress toward your main goal. When you successfully complete one long-term assignment, you'll feel more motivated to start the next one without procrastinating. Soon "I'm organized" might be one of your strengths!

I don't think I'm good enough

Hey Terra,

I'm just your average teen (maybe below average in looks). But all of the other average kids seem to have a lot more fun than I do. I do okay in school, but there's got to be more to life than getting good grades.

It would be so cool to have a bunch of friends to hang out with or to have a girlfriend, but I don't think I'm good enough for any girl to want to go out with me. Whenever I get the idea to call up someone, I stop myself because I'm sure no one would want to spend time with me. So I end up just staying home because the last thing I want to hear is somebody telling me they don't want to be with me. Even though they'd probably make up some polite excuse like "Sorry, I'm busy," I'd know what they really meant.

Why Bother?

Dear Why Bother,

It's normal to feel insecure at times, especially when you're going through a lot of changes (like puberty). But it sounds like you spend too much time putting yourself down. If you're always thinking, "I'm not good enough" and "Nobody wants to be with me," these put-downs become a habit, and it becomes hard to enjoy social situations—or life in general. Once you're aware of any bad habit, you can start gaining control of it.

Each time a negative thought about yourself pops into your head, notice it—but don't agree with it or get angry with yourself for thinking it. Instead, ask yourself what triggered the thought (a certain person, event, or situation, for example). Then come up with a positive thought to tip the scale in the other direction. If your automatic negative thought is, "Nobody likes me," replace it with something like, "My friends care about me." The goal is to get out of the habit of putting yourself down.

You can also raise your self-esteem by focusing on your strengths instead of your weaknesses. You said that you're a good student. Why not get involved in an academic club or volunteer to tutor other students who need help? These are ways to meet new people who are likely to respect and even admire you.

Insecurity can lead you to build a wall between yourself and the rest of the world, rather than risk being rejected. The wall keeps other people out, making it hard for them to get to know you (and vice versa). If you're ready for a change, break down the wall and reach out to others. Try starting a conversation with someone you don't know that well. Not everyone you meet will automatically become a friend, but some will, and that's worth a lot!

In friendship,
Terra

Loneliness

There's a big difference between being "alone" and being "lonely." Alone means by yourself, on your own. It's not a bad thing; in fact, most of us need some alone time occasionally. Being by ourselves can be fun, because it allows us to pursue special interests or hobbies. And it gives us a chance to get in touch with our deepest thoughts and our dreams of the future.

Being on your own is also about exploring your independence out in the world. Part of growing up is learning to be comfortable on your own and enjoying the freedom to decide what's right for you. Activities that don't involve your family give you a way to define yourself as an individual.

Loneliness, on the other hand, is about feeling left out, invisible, or disconnected from others. You can feel lonely all by yourself or in a room full of people. Either way, being lonely is never fun and can be very painful.

You might feel lonely if your best friend moves away or if the two of you drift apart. Or if you break up with your boyfriend/girlfriend. Or if you go to a new school and don't know anyone yet. Or if you're on a family vacation and miss having your friends around. Sometimes you might feel lonely if you don't believe that anyone really understands you.

If you feel lonely, it's normal to want to retreat from the world, but this never helps. Instead, make the effort to reach out to someone (even though it may be scary for you to do that). As the saying goes, "If something isn't scary, then it doesn't take real courage to do it." So be brave and go for it!

To get started, talk to someone in your class who seems friendly and invite this person to do something with you outside of school. Call a friend you've lost touch with. Volunteer at a child-care center or at a home for senior citizens. Or visit the teen chat rooms at Talk City's The InSite *(www.talkcity.com/the insite/chat/)*. There are plenty of ways to reach out—maybe you can think of a few more.

Connecting with others will help lessen the loneliness. At first, it might feel awkward to talk to other people, but try it anyway. Developing social skills takes practice, so don't worry if things don't go smoothly right away. If you still feel uncertain and you want to talk to someone about your loneliness, go to an adult you trust (a parent, teacher, school counselor, or religious leader, for example). Find someone who will be understanding and helpful.

On weekends, it's like I live on a deserted island

Hey Terra,

Sometimes I feel like I live on a deserted island when I'm not in school. The thing is, nobody ever wants to hang out with me on weekends or during vacations. What should I do?

Lonely

Dear Lonely,

Do you call other people and invite them over, or do you wait for them to call you? Maybe all you need to do is make the first move. Have a party or invite someone over to watch videos. Or, on a Friday afternoon, ask some people what their plans are for the weekend. If they mention a group activity and seem open to inviting others, ask if you can join them.

If you're not comfortable with either of these ideas, extend your school day by getting involved in extracurricular activities like sports, theater, dance, or community service. That way, you'll be doing things that interest you, as well as filling your lonely hours. These new activities will lead to new friends. Best of luck!

In friendship,
Terra

Sadness

Sadness can creep up slowly like fog or knock you over like a sudden explosion. When you're sad, you may feel teary, vulnerable, empty, or lost. You may want to be alone to cry, take a shower, spend time with your pet, write in your journal, or lie on your bed and listen to music. You might want to call up a friend, send an email, or seek comfort from your family.

There's no "right" way to deal with sadness. Different people cope with emotions in different ways. But if you're feeling sad, here are five steps you can take to help yourself feel better:

1. Figure out why you're sad. Sadness is usually the result of a loss of some sort. For example, if your parents separate or get divorced, you lose the family life you've always known. If you move to a new neighborhood, you lose people and places you care about. Even a change like the end of the school year— something you probably look forward to—can cause feelings of sadness as you leave behind favorite teachers, classes, and classmates. Disappointment can lead to sadness, too. To pinpoint the cause of your sadness, ask yourself these questions: Who or what have I lost? What changes have taken place in my life, and what have I lost as a result? Who has disappointed me? Have I disappointed myself?

2. Talk to someone you trust. You don't need someone to try to fix things for you, because you can do that yourself once you've figured out what's going on. But it does help to talk with someone you trust. When you're sad, it's comforting to share your feelings with someone who cares enough to listen.

3. Write down your feelings. Writing allows you to express your emotions, instead of keeping them trapped inside. It also helps you see your problems from a new perspective, which might lead to solutions. If your sadness is due to the loss of a relationship, write a letter to the person you've lost—the letter is for you to keep and *not to send*. As you write, notice how you feel. Read your writing aloud when you're done. How do you feel afterward?

4. Check in with your body. How do you feel physically? Are you hungry, thirsty, tired, or premenstrual? Overactive hormones or a lack of food, water, exercise, fresh air, or sleep can intensify your emotions. If you're feeling sad, pay attention to your physical needs and take care of your body. This will help you feel better physically *and* emotionally.

5. Try a change of scenery. Sometimes staring at the same four walls makes you feel stuck in your sadness. Getting outdoors and breathing fresh air helps. Make plans with someone you enjoy spending time with. Seeing new sights or having something to look forward to may raise your spirits.

Sometimes sadness is really more than sadness. When the feelings are very deep and hard to shake, they may be a symptom of depression. Depression hangs over you like a dark cloud that won't go away, and you may feel hopeless and unmotivated—as though you'll never be happy again. You may have trouble sleeping or feel as if you can't get up to face a new day. You may even have thoughts of hurting yourself or committing suicide.

If you feel depressed or suicidal, *get help right away.* Talk to a trusted adult immediately. You don't have to face this alone! There are people who care and want to help you feel better. Remember, you deserve to be happy, and you can be.

When Nothing Matters Anymore: A Survival Guide for Depressed Teens by Bev Cobain, R.N.,C. (Minneapolis: Free Spirit Publishing Inc., 1998). Are you feeling helpless, sad, lonely, angry, or unhappy? This book can help you figure out if you're depressed. First-person stories of young people with depression let you know you're not alone and you can find the help you need.

Covenant House Nineline

1-800-999-9999

www.covenanthouse.org

The nineline offers immediate support and referrals for young people who need help. Their crisis intervention hotline is open twenty-four hours a day, seven days a week.

Youth Work Links and Ideas

www.youthwork.com

This site lists many toll-free crisis hotlines, both nationwide and worldwide. No matter where you are, you can talk to someone who cares and is trained to help.

My grandma died, and I feel lost without her

Hey Terra,

My grandmother died last week. She had been sick for about a year and was having a lot of trouble breathing. So, in a way, it's better for her because she's not in pain anymore, but I still miss her! She had a great smile and would always listen to me no matter what I talked to her about.

The last time I saw her, she joked around, and even though she was very weak and had all these tubes stuck in her, she asked me how I was doing! I think she was the only person who really understood me. Now that she's gone, I feel really lost.

I used to write poems to her for her birthday, and she really liked them. I recently wrote a poem for her, but she died before I got to read it to her. I feel empty inside, and I don't want to talk to anyone.

Empty

Dear Empty,

I'm so sorry to hear about your grandma. Even though you know she isn't suffering anymore, you still miss her, of course. She really cared about you, and you made her life brighter, too. You gave each other something wonderful, and nothing can ever take that from you.

People deal with grief and loss in their own way and in their own time. Right now, you're feeling sad and lost and empty. This is normal, and so is feeling like you don't want to talk to anybody. But talk anyway, because it will help you feel better.

Who else in your family felt especially close to your grandma? Maybe you and that person can comfort each other by sharing your feelings, talking about her, and remembering the good times. If you can't talk to anyone at home, get in touch with your school counselor or another caring adult. If you lock your feelings inside, they'll keep hurting more and more.

I would also encourage you to continue writing poetry, which is a wonderful way to express yourself. Or write a letter to your grandma, saying all of the things you're feeling; this will make you feel closer to her. Keep this letter to yourself, if you want, or share it with someone else.

Because I believe that people who love us are always with us inside, I feel strongly that your grandma is there for you in your heart. If you ever need her advice, just find a quiet place and "talk" to her inside your head (you could even read your poems to her). Her love and wisdom are still there for you and always will be. Take care.

In friendship,
Terra

HOW YOU FEEL ABOUT YOUR LOOKS

Many teens spend a lot of time agonizing about their looks. Are you one of them? Maybe you love the way you look and wouldn't change a thing. It's great when you feel that way. But maybe you think you're not good-looking enough, muscular enough, tall enough, thin enough, "perfect" enough . . . Well, *enough already!* If you constantly compare yourself to other people or to images in magazines, movies, and on TV, you'll probably feel inadequate. You need to know that "good-looking" comes in all different sizes, shapes, and colors. Instead of reminding yourself (and everyone else) about your so-called flaws, focus on your good points. This is the first step to building a healthier relationship with your body.

Whenever you have a negative thought about your looks ("My rear end is too big," "My shoulders aren't broad enough," or "I hate my hair," for example), STOP. Don't put yourself down. Instead, practice replacing negative thoughts with positive ones. Find at least one thing that you like about your body or looks ("I have nice eyes," "My legs are strong," or "I like my smile," for example). Every time you have the urge to be self-critical, remember your good points instead.

Most people don't know this, but negative body thoughts often have more to do with how you *feel* than how you *look*. Consider how you typically deal with your emotions—do you express them in healthy ways, or do you hide them, ignore them, or shove them aside? If you don't express your feelings, where do you think they end up? Lots of times they get buried inside you and become more intense.

Because unexpressed feelings stick around for so long, it's easy to forget what originally caused them and to lash out at the closest target: your body. You may criticize yourself, diet too much, eat too much, work out excessively, or try other unhealthy ways of coping. If this sounds familiar, get in touch with what you're *really* feeling (because feeling "fat," for example, isn't an actual emotion). Here are four steps for improving your relationship with your body:

1. Wake up to media madness. Contrary to what advertisers want you to believe, people do *not* have perfect bodies, hair, teeth, skin, clothes, and so on. Don't buy into the hype. Be aware that models and celebrities who look "perfect" are often so thin that their health is in danger. Also, to achieve their glamorous image, they have to rely on lighting experts, hair and makeup artists, plastic surgeons, and computer wizards to make them look more beautiful. Think about it, how many people do you know who really look "perfect"?

2. Don't strive for perfection—it doesn't exist. Going after perfection wastes your time and creative energy. If you set impossible standards for your appearance, you'll always feel as if you don't measure up. No human being is perfect. The people who really love us accept the imperfect parts of us. To love yourself, you need to do the same thing.

3. What's behind the negative thinking? Every time you have a negative thought about your body, ask yourself, "What am I feeling right now?" Suppose you're getting ready to go to a dance. You look in the mirror and think something like, "No one would ever want to dance with someone who has such a big nose!" Stop and ask yourself what you're *really* feeling. Perhaps you're nervous about asking someone to dance with you, or you're worried that the person you like won't show up. See how it works? Most of the time, what you're feeling has nothing to do with your body.

4. Spread the word. Talk with your friends about the "perfect body" myth that the media is selling. Help them understand that when they criticize their bodies or obsess about their appearance, it's a sign that they're feeling something they haven't expressed yet. Be a role model by not criticizing yourself or comparing yourself to others. Make a point of talking to your friends about their feelings and complimenting them on their positive personality traits. Shifting the focus from looks to feelings and personal qualities will improve your relationship with your body, yourself, and others.

I want to look like the models in the fashion magazines

Hey Terra,

Okay, so I'm not great looking like the girls in the fashion mags. It's not like I don't try! What's wrong with me? Maybe I just like food too much to be thin and beautiful like my best chum who never eats anything. I'd like to be sexy like her, but I just can't, so it's no wonder no guys fancy me.

British Fat Girl

Dear British Girl,

First, stop thinking of yourself as "fat." Many girls and women are obsessed with their weight, and this isn't healthy. Good physical and emotional health is what it's really all about (not the number on the bathroom scale or the size of your jeans). Make an appointment with your doctor and have a checkup. Talk to him/her about the foods you eat, your activity level, and your family's health history. That way, you'll find out whether you need to make some changes in how you eat and exercise. The goal is to maintain good health.

Bodies come in different sizes. You may not be the same size as your friend or the fashion models, but this doesn't mean there's something "wrong" with you. In fact, you may be healthier than your friend, because we all need to eat food to be healthy and, as you say, *you actually eat and she doesn't!* (Is there a chance that your friend has an eating disorder? If so, she needs help. Talk to her or a trusted adult about the situation.)

Do yourself a favor: put away the fashion magazines and pick up a book about body image and health. This will help you understand your relationship with your body and feel more positive about who you are. When you feel good about yourself, your confidence increases and people want to get to know you. Learning to accept yourself and showing others what you have to offer is definitely a worthwhile goal. Thanks for writing.

In friendship,
Terra

The Invisible Woman by W. Charisse Goodman (Carlsbad, CA: Gurze Books, 1995). The author explores cultural discrimination against fat women. She shatters stereotypes, raises awareness about fat phobia and harassment, and states that no one has the right to discriminate against anyone based on their size and shape.

The Right Moves: A Girl's Guide to Getting Fit and Feeling Good by Tina Schwager, P.T.A., A.T.,C., and Michele Schuerger (Minneapolis: Free Spirit Publishing Inc., 1998). This book covers what teen girls need to know about eating right, exercising safely and effectively, and feeling good about themselves.

When Women Stop Hating Their Bodies: Freeing Yourself from Food and Weight Obsession by Jane R. Hirschmann and Carol H. Munter (New York: Fawcett Books, 1997). The authors explain how "bad body thoughts" are clues to your emotions, plus how to accept your body and treat it well.

About-Face

www.about-face.org

Here's help for losing a negative body image. This Web site educates girls and guys about the way the media has influenced views about what's "beautiful" and made so many people unhappy with their appearance.

"Problems with Food," The InSite

www.talkcity.com/theinsite/me/some_body/health/eating_disorders_alias.html

This section of Talk City's The InSite explores anorexia, bulimia, and compulsive overeating. A special feature includes "Been There" stories by young people who have struggled with eating disorders and won their battles.

My breasts are too big!

Hey Terra,

I have large breasts, and I hate them. I'm so sick of guys who look at my breasts instead of at me! It also really bugs me that guys think that because I'm big I'm automatically a slut. I can't help it if I'm big, and it doesn't make me a slut!

Screaming

Dear Screaming,

I don't blame you for your anger and frustration. Any guy who looks at your breasts instead of your face isn't treating you with respect and needs to be told, "Hey! I'm up here!" If the guys you encounter hear this often enough, they'll get the message.

Why do some guys act this way? It might have to do with media messages. Images of women's breasts are everywhere—on TV and billboards, and in movies, magazines, and arcade games. The message is that women with large breasts are attractive, sexy, and alluring. Some guys get the message and think it's acceptable to gawk at a girl's chest (an extremely rude thing to do). Girls get these messages, too, and may (wrongly) come to believe that their breast size determines their value.

You say that you hate your breasts because they're too big. Breast size is determined by heredity, and there's not much you can do about it (aside from plastic surgery, which I don't recommend, except to correct medical conditions). It's important for you to love and accept your body and to realize that you're much more than just a physical being. Your talents and goals count for a whole lot more than your breast size! Take care.

In friendship,
Terra

Would a popular girl ever like a chunky guy?

Send

Hey Terra,

There's this girl I think I'm in love with. She's really pretty, and she's friendly to everyone, especially guys, but she's also friendly to me. She sits next to me in Spanish, and she always says hi and asks me how I did on tests and stuff. When I see her in the hall, she smiles at me and waves. This is really amazing because I'm not good-looking or anything. In fact, I'm kind of chunky, and girls don't ever pay attention to me (except to make fun of me). Anyway, I'm thinking of buying her something special for Valentine's Day, but I'm not sure what she'll say.

Is She the One?

Dear Is She the One,

I understand that this girl's attention makes you feel good, but do you really know her well enough to be in love with her? What do you know about her personality and interests? It's normal to like someone who's friendly and pays attention to you, especially when you're feeling insecure about yourself. But if the girl in your Spanish class acts toward you the way she does toward a lot of other guys, it might just mean that she's outgoing. I suggest that you try to learn more about her before confessing your feelings.

For Valentine's Day, just give her a friendly card (not the romantic kind) and see what happens. If she's still friendly, talk with her and get to know her better. Let her see all of your positive qualities, and don't focus so much on your looks and your weight. If you're worried about your weight, you could talk to your doctor about it. Find out if you need to make some changes in the way you eat or in your activity level. But to answer your question, my guess is that a girl *would* go out with a "chunky" guy if she liked him for who he was.

There's one thing you need to know: the better you feel about yourself, the more likely it is that you'll find a girl to have a healthy relationship with. I wish you well.

In friendship,
Terra

MAKING DECISIONS

As you get older, you get to make more decisions about everything—what you wear, what classes you take, who you spend time with, who you date (if you date), where you go on weekends, what you do there, and more. Being responsible for your own decisions can be a mixed blessing. It's very satisfying to have more control over your life. But when life gets complicated and choices are hard, you might miss the days when your mom or dad decided everything for you.

When faced with a decision, do you tend to overanalyze everything and have a difficult time choosing? Or do you jump into things without considering the consequences first? Maybe you're somewhere in between? Or maybe you decide things differently depending on the situation. Whatever your usual decision-making style is, here's an exercise that can help you improve:

 You've been offered two summer jobs—one as a server at a fast-food restaurant and one as a counselor at a children's day camp. You have to decide by the end of the week, or you lose both opportunities. Which choice is right for you?

Decision-making can be difficult, but in this situation, as with any decision, you can start by writing down the pros and cons of each choice. For example:

FAST-FOOD RESTAURANT

Pros	Cons
– free shakes	– being inside
– decent pay	– being on my feet all day
– flexible work schedule	– being around greasy food
– lots of teens around	

CAMP

Pros	Cons
– working with little kids	– lower pay
– being outdoors	– little kids can be challenging
– swimming on the job	– not as many other
– will look good on résumé	teens around

When you review your lists, don't just compare the number of items in each column. Instead, consider how important each pro or con is to you. Maybe you love being outside, which you'll get plenty of at the camp. Notice that one of the cons of working at the fast-food place is that you're inside all day. This might push you in the direction of the camp job. On the other hand, maybe you're saving money for college, in which case better pay could steer you in the direction of the fast-food job. Weigh the pros and cons until the right choice becomes clear.

What happens if you're still not sure what to do? Talk to people you trust, find out if they've ever faced a similar decision, and ask for their advice—they may offer ideas you hadn't considered. Although it's your decision, it's sometimes helpful to hear other opinions and get a different point of view. In the end, you may have to listen to your inner voice or follow your gut feeling about which choice is right for you.

If you still can't decide, try one of these strategies:

• **Be tough with yourself.** Set a deadline for making the decision and stick to it. For example, tell yourself you've got only one day to decide. Think about the decision as much as you want that day. When your deadline arrives, keep your promise to decide and follow through no matter what.

• **Sleep on it.** Before you go to bed, say to yourself, "I will wake up tomorrow knowing what to do." This way, your mind can work on the problem while you're asleep. You might even have a dream that helps you decide. (Write down the dream the moment you wake up, so you don't forget it. Then think about what the dream might be telling you.)

Maybe you're afraid of making a poor choice. If so, ask yourself what's the worst that can happen. Sometimes making the "wrong" choice isn't a big deal. (You're out to eat and choose the salad instead of the sandwich, and you don't enjoy your meal—not a major catastrophe.) But sometimes a wrong decision *is* a big deal. (You decide you don't want to play soccer anymore, so you quit the team. Halfway through the season, you're bored and you miss the game and your teammates. *Now* what do you do?) If you're worried about not making the right decision, remember:

1. Things don't always turn out as planned. That's part of life and not necessarily a bad thing. Life's surprises can prove very interesting!

2. Every experience is a learning opportunity. Mistakes offer great opportunities for learning, even if it's only to learn what *not* to do next time.

3. Accept what is and make the best of the situation. There's no use getting upset about the things you can't change. Realizing that there's an "up" side to almost everything makes life easier and helps you move on to your next learning opportunity.

Isn't it MY decision?

Send▷

Hey Terra,

In the past, I've had some problems with low self-esteem and stuff. I couldn't talk to my parents about what was going on, and they got all worried and wanted me to talk to the school counselor. Well, I did talk to her, and she turned out to be really cool! So after a few months of going to her every week, I started feeling much better about myself.

But here's the problem—my family is moving next month, and I'm going to another school. My parents want me to meet regularly with the counselor at the new school, but I don't really think I need a counselor anymore. (I probably wouldn't even like him.) I feel like it's my decision, but my parents are really pressuring me. What should I do?

Cured

Dear Cured,

It's great that you don't think you need counseling anymore. Sounds like you're feeling much better about yourself! I agree that it needs to be your decision whether to talk to a counselor. But before you decide, make sure you have all of the facts. Have you met the new school counselor yet? If not, you can't really say whether you'd like him or not.

Also, keep in mind that going to a new school could be stressful at first. Until you find new friends, some of your old feelings of low self-esteem might return. If that happens, it would help to have someone to talk to—someone who really knows how to listen.

My advice is to talk to your current counselor and get her opinion, and then see how you feel when you get to the new school. It can't hurt to pop in and say hi to the new counselor. That way, if it turns out you do need to talk sometime, you'll already know who he is and he'll know you. Good luck!

In friendship,
Terra

How far should I go for a friend?

Send

Hey Terra,

I have a friend I've gotten pretty close to over the past year. He's cool, and we have a good time playing video games and hanging out. We're also on the same soccer team. The thing is, he's not that great of a student and I am. Lately, especially in math and science, he's been asking me to give him the answers to homework and tests. We're in the same science class, but I have math before lunch and he has it right afterward. The math teacher always gives the same exact tests and assignments to each class, which is one reason my friend wants to get my answers.

The first time he asked me for the answers, I didn't want to give them to him, but instead of telling him no, I pretended I didn't remember any of the questions. The next time, he really begged me, so I just kind of gave him part of the answer to one question.

We're having a big math test on Friday, and my friend wants me to write down all of the questions and give them to him right after my class finishes taking the test. I really don't want to do this, but I'm pretty sure if I don't, it's going to hurt our friendship. I don't know what to do!

Good Student

Dear Good Student,

Sometimes it's hard to stand up for what you believe in and act against a friend's wishes. I think you know exactly what the right thing to do is, but it's normal to have mixed feelings in this situation. Your friend knows he's asking you to cheat: what kind of friend would put you at risk like this? If he gets caught, you'll both be in trouble. Even if you don't get caught this time, he may keep asking you to cheat.

Although you don't want to risk your friendship, I suggest that you tell your friend how you honestly feel about the cheating. Let him know what your values are and why you want to stick to them. Offer to help him study, so he can get better grades on his own. If he doesn't want to be your friend after you tell him you won't cheat, that's his choice. He may actually be a "friend" you're better off without. You may feel hurt at first, but imagine how you'll feel if you don't do what you know is right. Setting aside your own values to please someone else won't lead to a healthy relationship—with your friend or with yourself. Best of luck!

In friendship,
Terra

CHAPTER 2

What Are Boyfriend/Girlfriend Relationships All About?

When you're eight, finding out that someone "likes" you might be enough to make you gag. At that age, romance isn't likely to be on your mind. Then sometime during your preteen and teen years, when your body starts changing, your thoughts might start changing, too. Almost overnight, the idea of having a boyfriend/girlfriend (bf/gf) may become so exciting that you can hardly think of anything else.

Many girls and guys think that having a bf/gf is part of what being a teen is all about. While it's true that the intense emotional waves you ride as an adolescent can lead to attractions to other people and to romantic relationships, this doesn't always happen. What if you're one of the millions of teens who has never been in love or had a bf/gf? Does this mean there's something wrong with you? No! Should you be worried? Absolutely not.

Almost everyone falls in love at least once in his/her life. If you haven't yet (but you want to), there's an excellent chance you will someday. Can you make it happen sooner? Probably not. But there *is* something you can do in the meantime: be clear about the things you want and need, which makes you more open to having them in your life. Being aware of what's important to you encourages you to look for what you want. This, in turn, helps you see the potential in situations and take advantage of opportunities that may result in new friendships . . . or even love.

LOOKING FOR LOVE

By now, you're responsible enough to leave the house alone, meet friends, and go places with them, and being independent like this is pretty cool (after all, it wasn't so long ago that you couldn't go anywhere without adult supervision). Maybe you love your freedom and independence, and you're not on the look-out for a romantic relationship. If so, being "single" isn't a problem for you, and in fact, you may love it.

But for some teens, being single *is* a major problem. Maybe you feel lonely and incomplete without a boyfriend/girlfriend, or as if something's missing from your life. If this sounds like you, you're probably wondering when you'll finally meet that special someone. Maybe you spend a lot of time dreaming about and searching for love.

Many teens (and preteens) spend *a lot* of energy obsessing about falling in love. Teens who constantly talk about how they *need* a bf/gf may be feeling pressured from articles in teen magazines or images on TV and in movies. Some young people believe they'll be cooler or more accepted if they're in a romantic relationship, and some just want a bf/gf because other people have one. No matter what the reason, teens who get into romantic relationships too soon usually aren't ready for them.

What most teens *really* need are opportunities to develop healthy friendships with girls and guys. If you think friends aren't as important as boyfriends/girlfriends, you're wrong! Friendships, in the long run, are often more meaningful and lasting than romantic relationships. You're probably more relaxed, open, and trusting with your friends, because you know and understand each other well, and the bond between you is strong. Romantic relationships, on the other hand, may be based more on physical attraction than common interests. Sometimes it's hard for young people in such relationships to build trust.

What's all this leading up to? If you have a boyfriend/girlfriend, be sure to still make time for your friends (not to mention your family and yourself). If you don't have a bf/gf, stop thinking of yourself as a lonely person looking for love—and start being a loving person who's busy living life.

Is my true love someone exactly like me?

Hey Terra,

In the movies, you can always tell when people meet their true love for the first time because they look at each other in this special way, like they recognize each other even though they've never met before. I know that things are different in real life, but is meeting your true love the same as falling in love at first sight? Is it like meeting someone who is so totally like you that they are your other half?

Waiting to Fall in Love

Dear Waiting to Fall in Love,

You're right, life isn't like the movies, although it's fun to imagine what it would be like if it was! In real life, people do fall in love "at first sight," but what they're probably feeling is a strong physical attraction. This may or may not develop into love.

I don't think that you can *truly* love someone you don't yet know. And how can you *know* someone you're meeting for the first time? You may love the way someone looks, but this isn't the same as *love*. Relationships grow as people discover their similarities and learn to respect and appreciate their differences. Someone who's totally like you (if there is such a person) isn't someone you can learn from or teach anything to. So how can the relationship grow?

Here's my advice: don't waste time waiting to fall in love. Get to know yourself better by exploring your interests and developing friendships. In the process, you may get close to people who are nothing like you, which will offer you a chance to learn and grow. I wish you well.

In friendship,
Terra

I wish I had a girlfriend!

Hey Terra,

I feel very lonely these days. I wish I had a girlfriend like every other guy I know. When I see guys my age with their arms around a girl laughing and talking, it just looks so perfect. I've got guys I'm good friends with, but having a girlfriend would really be the best.

Lonely Guy

Dear Lonely Guy,

Most people feel lonely at times, even if they're in a romantic relationship. Of course, having someone special to share your life with is a wonderful thing, and part of what a healthy relationship gives you is a sense of belonging.

It sounds like you already know how to be a good friend, and this is one of the "people skills" you need to find a girlfriend. But until she comes into your life, don't worry so much about the romantic side of your relationship with girls. Instead, find some girls to be friends with and start enjoying the company of females this way. Friendships are natural and relaxed, and romances that develop from them have a healthy foundation. Thanks for writing.

In friendship,
Terra

I need a boyfriend!

Hey Terra,

I'm fifteen, and all my friends have had boyfriends nonstop since the sixth grade. But I've never even had *one,* and it's driving me crazy! I read a lot of teen magazines, and I know a lot about hair and makeup and cool clothes. I try to look good, and I think I *do,* it's just that no guys seem to notice. I've also read a lot about how to "catch" a guy, but nothing I do seems to work.

Needs a Boyfriend

Dear Needs a Boyfriend,

Right now, it's harder (but definitely not impossible!) for you to be happy as a single girl when all your friends have boyfriends. I understand that you want to be like your friends in many ways and to share their experiences. I would suggest, however, that you don't spend too much energy worrying about attracting guys and finding romance. Although the magazines you're reading may focus on how to look good and "catch" a guy, there are more important things to concentrate on—like who you really are and what you want to do with your life. Take the time to develop your character, your strengths, and your talents. Without your unique personality, all you become is a face and a body. What's the point of being a girl who's part of a couple if you're nothing on your own?

I know that finding a boyfriend seems very important right now, but my experience tells me that things happen when they're supposed to. Instead of being preoccupied with the search for love, work on becoming a more complete person. Someone who "needs" to be part of a couple to be happy may be missing some essential pieces of self, such as self-esteem, self-respect, self-reliance, and self-confidence. When you develop these qualities, you'll have more to offer in a relationship. You'll also be preparing yourself for being on your own as an adult.

Widen your circle of friends by finding some single girls and guys to hang out with. And make sure that when you and your girlfriends are together, you agree not to spend all your time talking about guys and how to find love. Instead, talk about ways to become stronger, more independent young women. You're worth it!

In friendship,
Terra

I've looked everywhere for a boyfriend

Hey Terra,

Why can't I find a boyfriend? I've looked EVERYWHERE!

Searching

Dear Searching,

Boyfriends aren't lying around like lost quarters on the sidewalk, waiting for someone to find them. They're people living lives, which is exactly what you need to do, too. You're a valuable, interesting person with or without a boyfriend. Relax and stop looking for love.

Once you do, you'll have extra time and energy, so why not put it to good use? The world is filled with wonderful things to get involved in: theater, art, sports, community service, writing, and more. Find something that interests you, and you'll meet people. You can count on it!

In friendship,
Terra

I always like guys I can't get

Hey Terra,

My problem is this: the guys I always fall in love with are ones I can't get because they already have girlfriends or they're super-popular and out of my league. Why do I keep doing that? Also, I read a lot of romance novels, and I dream about the guys in the books or about movie stars. In the dreams, these guys always fall in love with me at first sight and I totally fall in love with them. I know there's not much chance that I'll ever meet Leonardo DiCaprio or Brad Pitt, so why do I keep dreaming about them?

Silly Tilly

Dear Silly Tilly,

Maybe you fall for guys who are attached or otherwise unavailable (like fictional characters and movie stars) because you're not ready for a romantic relationship, except inside your head. By fantasizing the entire relationship, you completely control both sides of it. This isn't necessarily a bad thing. Many people use fantasies or dreams to understand their emotions and to practice what they would do in real-life situations.

Another possibility is that you don't believe that you're good enough to be in a relationship with the guys you have crushes on. This is a self-esteem issue, and you might want to talk to a school counselor about it. If you want to work on your self-esteem, consider getting involved in a sport, a service project, or another challenging activity, which can help you feel good about yourself and your personal skills. Sports, activities, and hobbies (other than reading romance novels!) can help you focus less on falling in love and more on making yourself the best person you can be. Thanks for writing.

In friendship,
Terra

LOVE VS. LUST

What is love? No one has it completely figured out. That feeling we call love remains magically mysterious because it's different for everyone. Plus, there are many kinds of love: love for a parent, a close relative, a best friend, a sports hero (that's admiration), a mentor (that's gratitude), a total stranger in need (that's compassion), and so on. Then you have the stuff that poets and songwriters have tried to describe for centuries: the ever-intoxicating, pump-up-your-heart-with-"joy juice," got-to-have-it *romantic* love. That's the feeling you get when you think you're with "the one." The one you love may not actually *be* "the one," but you believe he/she is until you discover otherwise.

So when you've found that special someone, are you feeling love or is it simply *lust* (an intense physical attraction)? Figuring out the difference can be difficult because intense physical feelings are hard to separate from intense emotions. Love includes feelings of contentment, affection, attraction, and belonging, plus a connection with and concern for each other. Mature adult love may include commitment and a desire to build a lasting partnership and perhaps a family. For teens, love is often about being with someone you're attracted to and who understands and appreciates you.

Lust, on the other hand, has to do with sexual drive. At this time in your life, your body is humming with hormones that come with growing up. These hormones create strong sexual feelings. Sexual feelings lead to sexual thoughts. The feelings are normal and so are the thoughts (they're part of being human).

But just because you have sexual thoughts about and feelings toward someone doesn't mean you need to act on them. You can explore the sexual thoughts through fantasies, writing, music, or art, and you can redirect sexual energy through sports, exercise, dance, or drama. You can also release sexual feelings through masturbation, if you feel okay about it. All of these are safe ways to lessen your sexual drive.

Why lessen it? Because the decision to have sex with someone isn't a simple one. Sex means more than doing something just because it "feels good." It feels good to take a hot shower after you've been out in the cold, or to get a hug from a friend when you're feeling down, or to eat ice cream just about anytime. But unlike these activities, the decision to have sex with someone is complicated, and a lot of people don't understand this until it's too late.

As a teen, you need to have all of the facts before deciding whether sex is right for you at your age. You may think you've got all the facts if you know about menstruation, ovulation, erection, ejaculation, conception, and pregnancy, and if you understand how to protect yourself against unwanted pregnancy and sexually transmitted diseases—including HIV. These *are* critical facts, and being ignorant of them can result in life-threatening consequences. If you need to know more about them, take a look at pages 93–99 in Chapter 4, "Sex, Unhealthy Romantic Relationships, and Good-byes." You can also check out the "Where to Turn" resources on page 100.

But as important as those "facts of life" are, you need to know *more*. Having all the facts about sex includes knowing the *emotional* facts of life. Take a look at pages 101–105 for lots more information about how having sex changes you, your feelings, and your relationships. This will help you determine what your values are when it comes to sex.

In the meantime, remember that while you may have sexual feelings for someone you love, don't assume that you "love" everyone you're sexually attracted to!

He says he loves me and wants to have sex

Hey Terra,

My boyfriend and I have been together for almost three weeks. He's really cute and sweet. He says he loves me, and he's ready to have sex with me! No one's ever told me that before. I like (not love) him, but I think I may be ready to have sex with him. I'm really curious about what it will be like. I've never even seen a penis before. But there's a part of me that's a little bit scared. What can I do to relax?

Curious

Dear Curious,

If relaxing means ignoring your doubts, don't relax! I think that curiosity is a very poor reason to have sex. There's too much at risk to take it so casually. Your boyfriend may be the cutest, sweetest guy in the world, but I seriously doubt that he knows you well enough in three weeks to love you. It sounds like he's confusing love with lust.

What's your rush to have sex with him? You say that you don't love him. Do you want to do it just because he wants to or because you're curious? It's perfectly natural to be curious about what a penis looks like, but why not just go to the library and check out some human anatomy books? That way, you can look all you want without risking pregnancy, sexually transmitted diseases (STDs), and emotional hurt.

Be honest with yourself. If you're scared about having sex, that's your inner voice telling you this isn't the right thing to do. Listen to it! Too many girls are willing to believe that they're ready to have sex because a guy says, "I love you." *You* are the only one who knows when you're ready. If you have sex with your boyfriend and the relationship ends (as 99.9 percent of all teen relationships do), you probably won't feel very good about yourself. Do what's best for *you*. Only you know what that is! Take care.

In friendship,
Terra

I feel guilty about what I did

Hey Terra,

There's this girl I know, and we hang out sometimes after cross-country practice (we've got a coed team). On Friday, she was wearing this really nice top and when we were talking after practice, she was standing much closer to me than normal. Well, after a while, she asked me if I wanted to touch her breasts. Of course I wanted to, but it didn't feel like the right thing to do. But she kept moving closer and saying stuff like, "What's the matter, are you afraid?" So I finally touched her, and she seemed to like it. Then she put her hand on my pants, you know, down there. I'll admit, it felt really good, but now I feel so guilty about it that I don't know if I should cut practice on Monday or what.

What Did I Do?

Dear What Did I Do,

It sounds like you're feeling guilty, because your inner voice told you not to do something but you did it anyway. You may also be a little angry at the girl you touched, because the pressure she put on you wasn't fair or respectful. Instead of cutting cross-country to avoid this girl, go to practice and give it your all. Afterward, talk to the girl about your feelings and let her know what your boundaries are.

Sexual activities may feel good on a physical level, but if you're unsure about whether they're right for you at this point in your life, you'll undoubtedly feel some guilt after the fact. Guilt stays with you longer than even the most pleasant physical sensations. This is why it's important to know your values and always listen to what your inner voice is telling you. I hope this helps!

In friendship,
Terra

How can we spend less time having sex?

Hey Terra,

I'm good friends with this guy, and we're really attracted to each other. Even though I love him as much more than a friend and we've had sex, he's made it really clear that I'm not the girl of his dreams. He's got some fairy-tale ideas about love, and he's so convinced that love has to be a certain way that he doesn't realize how special our relationship is.

Anyway, I'd really like to get to know him better and give him a chance to get to know me, so he can realize what I already know about our relationship. But the trouble is, whenever we're alone, all either of us ends up wanting to do is have sex. Do you have any ideas about how we can not do that so much so we can talk?

More Than Just Friends

Dear More Than Just Friends,

You seem to want more of an emotional connection with this guy. When two people haven't given themselves the time to get to know each other, sexual activity remains just that—an "activity." If you want something different for yourself in this relationship, talk to the guy about your feelings. This may not be easy. In fact, for lots of people, it's much easier to have sex than to talk about deep feelings and what sex actually means in the relationship.

Explain why a relationship based on more than physical attraction and sex is important to you. If you tell your friend that you want to spend more time together in nonsexual intimacy but he's not interested, you may discover that this relationship isn't meeting your emotional needs (and decide to end it). Good luck!

In friendship,
Terra

Is he up to something?

Hey Terra,

I just met a guy at a party. I'm fourteen, and he's sixteen. As soon as he saw me, he came over and started complimenting me on my looks and my clothes, and he said that he thought he was falling in love with me. Then he asked me if I liked sex. I told him I didn't know because I was a virgin. Then he kissed me in a real sexy way, and I couldn't think straight. Then he asked me out for this weekend. He said we could go to his friend's house because that kid's parents weren't going to be home. I haven't told him yes yet because I'm thinking he might be too old for me. Do you think he is, and do you think he's up to something?

Saturday Girl

Dear Saturday Girl,

I'm not as concerned about this guy's age as I am about his attitude toward girls and his behavior. You said you couldn't think straight after he kissed you, which is exactly what he wanted: a girl who wasn't thinking straight. This guy seems to be moving way too fast. I think it would be a mistake for you to go to his friend's house for several reasons:

1. You don't know this guy.
2. You have no reason to trust him.
3. He may be more interested in getting physical with you
   than getting to know you as a person.
4. Being alone with this guy could be dangerous.

If you're not convinced, talk to some girls who are no longer virgins and ask them about guys who only seem to want sex.

Here's another idea: if you *are* interested in this guy and you want to get to know him, invite him to go out with you and a group of friends. Find out if you have anything in common. If he seems sincere about his feelings for you, spend time getting to know him better.

You're smart not to rush into sex. Keep listening to your inner voice!

In friendship,
Terra

Make a Noise
www.makeanoise.ysp.org.au/
This Web site offers information on a variety of topics affecting teens, including mental and physical health, sex and relationships, and much more. You'll find lots of ideas for handling the stresses and pressures you face each day, plus advice on listening to your inner voice.

GETTING NOTICED

Sometimes looking for love isn't necessary because the person you want has already been found (she's in your history class, or he's your friend's cousin, for example). This person has all the qualities you've ever dreamed of in a boyfriend/girlfriend. You know just what you want and where to get it, so everything's cool, right? Not necessarily.

What if the person you like isn't aware that you exist? Or what if your "crush" knows you exist but has never actually said anything to you? What if you feel too shy or scared to talk to the person? Is there any hope for a relationship? Of course!

But nothing's going to happen unless you *make* it happen. If you want to change the situation, you're going to have to take action.

Have you ever noticed that certain people, no matter what they look like, always seem to get positive attention? Why is that? Probably because of their *self-confidence*. They smile, make eye contact, act friendly, and are genuinely interested in others. This makes other people feel comfortable around them.

If you're not feeling particularly confident, especially around someone you have a crush on, it's going to be harder to get the attention you want. (But not impossible!) You might have to push yourself out of your usual comfort zone and take a risk. Maybe the thought of saying hi to the person you like makes your throat dry and your palms sweaty. These reactions are normal when you're nervous. So, say hi anyway! Give yourself a chance to get to know the person you like, and give him/her a chance to get to know you.

Not so long ago, it was unusual for a girl to call up a boy or ask him out on a date. Guys did all the asking, while girls did all the waiting. Things have changed (and that's a good thing!), so girls as well as guys know how scary it is to make the first move. You can convince yourself that it will be like getting a tooth pulled without novocaine, or you can take a deep breath (don't forget to exhale!) and just walk up to the person and start talking. If you never make your feelings known, your crush might not notice you, and you might spend the rest of forever wondering what would have happened if only you'd had the nerve to say hi.

Look at it this way: you've got nothing to lose. If you let fear keep you from getting to know someone you like, you'll be left wondering "What if?" But if you make the effort to reach out to other people, all kinds of wonderful things might happen!

How can you tell if someone likes you?

Hey Terra,

My friends are always telling me that some girl likes me, but I don't know how they can tell when I can't! Is there a trick to knowing if someone likes you?

Wondering Guy

Dear Wondering Guy,

There are two ways to tell if a girl likes you:

1. Check her "body language." Does she smile when you look at her, or does she run away screaming? (Just kidding!) Does she act friendly or completely uninterested? Does she treat you differently than other people? Think of the ways you show people that you like them. You probably act friendly and interested in what they have to say. Does the girl you like act this way toward you?

Of course, some people hide their emotions, and it's hard to tell what they're really feeling. If you're interested in a girl and her behavior doesn't give you a clue about her feelings, try option 2.

2. Ask someone who knows the girl (make sure it's someone you trust) to find out whether she likes you. If the answer is yes, go talk to her. The conversation could be the beginning of a relationship.

If the answer is no, you may be disappointed that she doesn't feel the same way about you, but at least you're not left wondering. In these kinds of situations, you always have a choice. If you're still interested, you can reach out to this girl in friendship and see what develops over time. Or you can put your energy into your friends and hobbies. Or you can find another girl to ask out. This gives you the freedom to get on with your life. Good luck!

In friendship,
Terra

I'm too shy to talk to her!

Hey Terra,

I'm too shy to talk to the girl I have a crush on. I see her on the bus every day, and she's really friendly to everyone. It would be so easy to talk to her during the fifteen-minute ride to school, but I'm way too shy! What should I do so she'll notice that I'm interested?

Stressed

Dear Stressed,

You didn't mention whether shyness is a problem you have when talking to people in general or just this girl. If you're only shy with her, you're probably worried about making a good impression. Try a relaxation exercise, where you tense all your muscles while taking a slow, deep breath. Then relax your muscles as you breathe out slowly. Repeat this a few times.

Next, picture yourself approaching the girl you like and saying hi. Imagine her responding positively. You could even have an imaginary conversation with her when you're alone in your room. Don't plan every word you'll say. (When you really talk to her, you don't want to sound like you've memorized a script!) It's fine to think about an opening topic of conversation, such as a teacher, a class, or an activity you have in common.

Once you can comfortably talk to her in your imagination, start a conversation in real life. Sometimes getting over that first hello makes things a lot easier. Besides, if she's friendly, you won't have to do all the talking, and by listening, you'll get to know her better. Best of luck!

In friendship,
Terra

My dream guy already has a girlfriend! Send

Hey Terra,

I have definitely found my dream guy, but he's already got a girlfriend, so what should I do? It doesn't look like he's going to notice me or break up with his girlfriend anytime soon. They've been together for the whole six months I've loved him. Should I just be patient and wait for him to realize I'm the love of his life, or should I give up?

Really

Dear Really,

If you've waited six months for him to notice you, I'd say it's time to move on. Besides, it sounds like this guy cares a lot about the girl he's already with, which could explain why he has eyes only for her. A guy who's involved with someone else is unavailable in my opinion, so my best advice is to forget about him. The *right* dream guy will be as interested in you as you are in him—that's how you'll recognize him. And he'll be worth the wait! Take care.

In friendship,
Terra

ASKING SOMEONE OUT

Suppose you've found the courage to start a conversation with someone you like, and the two of you have become friends. Maybe now you like this person even more than before. What's your next move? You can ask him/her out.

Before you do this, be clear in your mind about what "going out" means. People in various parts of the country (and the world) have different words to describe phases of dating and relationships, but the explanations are essentially the same. Depending on where you live, asking someone to "go out" could mean (1) you like each other and you may or may not be willing to let other people know it, (2) you hang out together at lunch and in between classes, exchange notes, talk to each other on the phone, and send email, (3) you go places together as a couple within a larger group of friends, or (4) you go places as a couple, just the two of you—also called "dating." Some teens may "go out with" (or "go with") someone for only a few days, or hours, before the relationship ends.

Asking the person you like out on a real *date* involves more of an emotional risk. Planning the date is part of getting to know each other better, and the date itself is a way to find out whether you enjoy spending time together outside of school. In the planning stages, you have to decide whether to go to a movie or some other place, and you might have to get parental permission. You also need to decide on transportation and who pays for what. In other words, going on a real date takes more planning than simply writing notes or hanging out at school.

Going on a date with someone doesn't necessarily mean you're in a romantic relationship. Lots of people go on one date and choose not to go out together again, for whatever reason. To confuse matters, just because you're dating someone doesn't necessarily mean you can't also be dating other people. The important thing to remember is to keep the lines of communication open. Without making agreements about the relationship (for example, is it all right to see other people?), misunderstandings happen and feelings get hurt.

When two people have an agreement that neither of them will date anyone else, it's considered to be an *exclusive* relationship. In this type of relationship, the couple might go out on dates or just spend time together. Again, the ground rules for flirting or being sexual with someone outside of the relationship must be agreed upon ahead of time, so there's no confusion. If you're not ready for a serious relationship, consider dating casually, which means going on dates with people you're interested in but not committing to an exclusive relationship yet.

It can be scary to ask someone for a date, no doubt about that. Obviously, you want the person to say yes—but what if the answer's no? Will your feelings be hurt? Probably a little. Will you survive? Absolutely. Keep one thing in mind, and you'll get over the disappointment much faster: *Don't waste time longing for people who don't want to be in a relationship with you. The best boyfriends/girlfriends are the ones who like you as much as you like them. Forget about the rest.*

Dating offers no guarantees, but you can take steps to make the asking-out process a little easier. Here are a few tips that may help you get the answer you want:

1. Ask someone you know. It's less stressful to ask out someone you know, rather than a stranger. If you ask someone you don't know to go out with you, the odds of getting a yes are less than if you ask a person who already knows and likes you. Also, if you don't know the person you're going out on a date with, you might quickly discover that you don't really have much in common or enjoy spending time together. Then you're on a date that can feel awkward and *verrrrry* long.

2. Get friendly with the person first. There's nothing wrong with being attracted to someone you don't know, but just because the person you like is "hot" doesn't automatically mean that he/she would make a fun date or a great bf/gf. Take the time to get to know a person *before* you ask him/her out. (This gives the other person a chance to get to know and feel comfortable with *you*, too.) Once the two of you become friendly, or even close friends, you can decide whether you're interested in moving into the bf/gf zone. Remember, people who know and like each other as friends *first* stand a better chance of having a healthy romantic relationship than people who don't know each other at all.

3. Take a deep breath and go for it. You can never win if you're not willing to play the game. Dating is fun (it's definitely a learning experience), and it's a great opportunity to get out in the world and discover what's important to you in a relationship. So take the plunge and ask the big question, "Will you go out with me?"

I don't have the guts to ask a girl out

Hey Terra,

I really wish I had a girlfriend, but I've never had the guts to ask a girl out on a date. I'm starting to think I never will, and it's making me kind of depressed.

Scared

Dear Scared,

You don't say how old you are, and that makes a big difference in the advice I'd give. For example, a fourteen-year-old who's too shy to ask someone out may not have a problem at all; a twenty-year-old in the same situation might.

    I agree that it takes guts to ask a girl out. After all, she might say no, and in some ways, it can even be scary if she says yes! Still, you have to be ready to take the risk if you really want to date. You might not be ready to do this, and that's just fine. Some people are ready to date a lot earlier than others, and you have to decide what's right for you. To make things easier, I'd suggest you go out with a group of girls and guys who are friends, so there's less pressure. Relax and enjoy yourself. If you get to know girls as people—as friends—it will be easier to move forward from there. Take care.

In friendship,
Terra

What if she laughs at me?

Hey Terra,

I'm in love for the first time, but I'm so afraid that if I tell my girlfriend how deep my feelings are, she'll laugh (or worse) and I'll be shattered forever.

Fearful

Dear Fearful,

Sometimes, the fear of rejection is a lot scarier than rejection itself. What you need is the help of a trusted friend and a little time to practice saying the words you want to say, so you can build up your confidence.

Pretend that your friend is the girl you love. This will probably make both of you laugh, which will help loosen you up. Imagine lots of different ways to tell her how you feel. Be creative and have fun! (This kind of exercise is called role-playing, and it's a useful way to safely practice real-life situations that are difficult for you. Actors use a similar technique to help them get better at improvisation, a kind of spontaneous acting done without a script.)

Have your friend come up with a wide range of responses—everything from, "Get out of my face," to "I've been waiting for months to hear those words from you!" After you do this exercise a few times, you'll feel more confident about actually telling the girl how you feel. I hope you get the reaction you're looking for. Good luck!

In friendship,
Terra

How can I find out if she likes me?

Hey Terra,

I've had a crush on a girl for about two months, only I haven't had the nerve to ask her out yet. I wrote her three letters, but I still haven't heard from her. What should I do to find out if she likes me? How can I get her to go out with me?

Desperate

Dear Desperate,

Did you mail the three letters? If she got your letters and didn't respond, that's a sign that she's not interested in you romantically. If you still want to pursue her, I suggest you do something really brave: call her up and ask her out on a date. What's the worst that could happen?

If she turns you down, she turns you down. It might hurt, but at least you won't have to spend any more time wondering how she feels. Then again, maybe she'll say yes! I wish you luck!

In friendship,
Terra

He only likes me as a friend

Hey Terra,

I've been crazy about this guy for a while. I've even told him how I feel, but he says he only likes me as a friend. I like him so much more than that. What can I do to get him to change his mind?

Love Struck

Dear Love Struck,

It sounds like you've already *done* what you can do. You've told this guy how you feel, and he's told you the kind of relationship he wants with you for now. I know that it hurts to get rejected, especially when your feelings for someone are strong. Is there anyone you can talk to about this? Do you have ways to make yourself feel better? Get some exercise, spend time with friends, or focus on school and after-school activities. Maybe, in time, this guy's feelings for you will change, but it's best not to sit around waiting for that to happen. You've got better things to do with your time!

In friendship,
Terra

What do girls REALLY want?

Hey Terra,

I think about sex all the time, though I haven't had a girlfriend yet. Tell me, is it true that girls say they don't like guys to hit on them but they really do? I need to know this for the future because the girl of my dreams just moved into my neighborhood. I haven't talked to her yet, but I plan to ask her out!

Romeo to Be

Dear Romeo to Be,

I'm not sure whether you're talking about "hitting on" as in flirting or pressuring a girl for sex. It's risky to make a generalization about whether girls enjoy it when guys flirt a lot (some do, some don't). But if you want to know if girls like being pressured into things, the answer is a definite NO. Some guys think girls say no to play hard to get. This isn't true, so don't believe it. No means no.

So, "the girl of your dreams" is moving into your neighborhood? Cool! I often hear from teens who want to know how to make the big romantic step when they've never even had a conversation with the guy/girl of their dreams. I suggest that you take it slow and get to know this girl before you start planning your first kiss. Since she's new in town, she'll probably be glad to meet you, but you need to know her as a real person not a dream girl. Talk to her, spend time together, and see if you enjoy being around each other.

As for your sexual fantasies, they're normal, but just make sure that you keep them in your head, instead of acting them out on girls you don't know. A good boyfriend is someone who cares about and respects his girlfriend's wants and needs. Take care.

In friendship,
Terra

WHAT MAKES A "GOOD" BOYFRIEND/GIRLFRIEND?

Suppose you have all the close friends you need at the moment, but a part of you is still looking for a boyfriend/girlfriend. If you're searching for the "perfect" guy/girl, it's time for a reality check. No matter how great someone looks, sounds, and acts, *no one* is perfect. Movies, television, magazines, and romance novels may lead you to believe otherwise, but it's all just hype.

Here's the truth: there may be someone who's right for you, but this person may not at all resemble your mental image of your dream guy/girl. That's why it's important to determine what you're *really* looking for in a relationship. What makes someone a good match for *you?* To increase your chances of recognizing the right person when you meet, you have to know what you really want and need.

To find out what's important to you, create a "What Matters Most" list. It will help you sort out what you want in a bf/gf. Don't focus too much on *appearance* when you're making this list. Instead, think about personal qualities or strengths you admire in people. Once you have a clearer image of the characteristics you're looking for, it's easier to recognize a potential match. Plus, you'll be more likely to avoid relationships that have little chance of working out.

What Matters Most
Ten steps to finding what you want in a boyfriend/girlfriend

1. Get a pencil and some paper. You're going to make a couple of lists, and writing things down (not just keeping them in your head) makes this exercise more effective.

2. Fold the paper in half lengthwise. You'll now have room for two long columns.

3. At the top of the left-hand column, write this heading: "I want a boyfriend who . . ." or "I want a girlfriend who . . ."

4. At the top of the right-hand column, write this heading: "I *don't* want a boyfriend who . . ." or "I *don't* want a girlfriend who . . ."

5. Make the lists. Write down any qualities you're looking for in a bf/gf. You can write about personality traits, values, looks, or anything else. This list can be totally private, so don't hold back! The more detailed you make it, the better. You might be really surprised by some of your answers. Don't censor yourself; just write down anything, even if some items contradict others. There are no wrong answers here—whatever is true for you is the right answer. Besides, no one else will ever see this list, unless you choose to share it.

6. Keep brainstorming. Make the lists as long and as specific as you can, until you finally run out of ideas. After a while, your list might look like this:

I WANT A GIRLFRIEND WHO . . .	I DON'T WANT A GIRLFRIEND WHO . . .
– is available and wants a relationship with me	– has a bad temper
– is intelligent	– is into drugs or alcohol
– has a good sense of humor	– acts jealous
– is friendly	– is conceited
– cares about her looks but doesn't obsess over them	– is a total slob

7. Turn all of the negatives into positives. Look at your "don'ts" list and start changing the statements to positive "do's." This encourages you to focus on what you want, not on what you *don't* want. For example, you might change "I don't want a boyfriend who's possessive" to "I want a boyfriend who trusts me." After you've done this, cross out the negative statements. Transfer all your new "do's" to your left-hand column.

8. Get more specific. Review your list to see if any of your wants are vague. If you wrote, "I want a girlfriend who's nice," you're not being specific. What exactly does "nice" mean to you? (Your girlfriend calls you every night? Never breaks dates? Gives you gifts on special occasions?) Be specific if you want results; otherwise it's kind of like walking into a clothing store and telling the salesperson, "I want a shirt." Elaborate on your needs and then cross out the vague statements.

9. Prioritize the items on your list. Everything on your list isn't equally important. Some items rate as "This is a must!" Others are in the "Would be good but not essential" category. For example, if you'd like your bf/gf to be athletic (because you are and you want to share that), mark that item "This is a must!" If you think it would be cool to be involved with someone who's into the same music as you are, mark that item "Would be good but not essential." After you've prioritized your items, get a clean sheet of paper and make two new columns: one for "This is a must!" and the other for "Would be good but not essential." And while you're at it, number the items in order of importance. Mark what really matters *most* to you number 1. The next item of importance is ranked number 2. You get the idea.

10. Review your list. Look it over carefully. Does your list describe anybody you already know?

Before you go out into the world to find a boyfriend/girlfriend, you've got one more list to make. This one is called the "What I Have to Offer" list. Finding a good match involves not only knowing what you want but also what you bring to the relationship.

What I Have to Offer
Seven steps to being the other half of a great couple

1. Get a pencil and some paper.

2. Fold it in half lengthwise. You'll now have room for two columns.

3. At the top of the left-hand column, write this heading: "My strengths are . . ."

4. At the top of the right-hand column, write this heading: "My weaknesses are . . ."

5. Make the lists. Write your answers on both halves of the paper. Be totally honest because no one will see this but you, unless you want them to.

6. Keep brainstorming. Make the columns as long and as specific as you can, until you finally run out of ideas. After a while, your lists might look like this:

MY STRENGTHS ARE . . .	MY WEAKNESSES ARE . . .
–I'm affectionate	–I'm sometimes disorganized
–I'm cheerful	–I'm stubborn
–I'm smart	–I can be too sensitive
–I give good advice	–I get jealous
–I have good judgment	–I'm late a lot

7. Review your lists. Have you written all the strengths you can think of? Have you been too hard on yourself in terms of your weaknesses? Adjust your lists, if needed.

If you've completed both the "What Matters Most" and the "What I Have to Offer" lists, you've raised your level of awareness about what you're looking for in a bf/gf and what you have to offer in a relationship. That's a great start!

Defining what you're looking for doesn't guarantee that you'll find a good match right away, but it does take you one step closer. And being clear about what you want and what you have to offer makes it much easier to envision a future relationship, which in turn helps you make things happen.

Remember, it's smart to stay open to opportunities that come your way. As you get to know someone new, do a quick mental comparison with your list. Do you see any possibilities for a match? When you're aware of what you're looking for, you may suddenly meet lots of people who could be a good boyfriend/girlfriend for you. Does this mean there's some cosmic force at work? Well, it's more likely that you just have a more open mind. Maybe your lists helped you see that looks are much less important than the way a person treats you, for example. You might even start seeing people you already know in a whole new light!

Keep your lists handy and review them often. Feel free to make changes, too. Cross out or renumber items whenever you want and add new items as they come to you. If you find someone who has some of the important qualities on your list, get to know this person. But remember that no one's perfect. The best thing two people can do for each other is to acknowledge their strengths and help each other work on their weaknesses. This is how people, and relationships, grow.

I'm having trouble finding my type

Hey Terra,

I know exactly what my type is. She's 5 feet, 8 inches, she weighs 120 pounds, and she has long blond hair and great legs. I know we could be so happy. The problem is, I'm having trouble finding her.

Help!

Dear Help,

Are you saying that if you met a great girl who was petite and had brown hair, you wouldn't go out with her because she isn't your type?! By defining your type only in *physical* terms, you're totally limiting your options. You might overlook a potential girlfriend just because she doesn't fit your dream profile.

Put your ideas of beauty aside for a moment and make a list of what you're looking for in a relationship—without listing physical attributes. Focus on qualities you admire in people, such as being affectionate or trustworthy, or having a good sense of humor—whatever's important to you. After you make your list, start looking for girls who have some of these qualities. You might find yourself falling in love with someone who doesn't resemble what you thought your type was. Life can be full of all kinds of pleasant surprises! Thanks for writing.

In friendship,
Terra

Am I too picky?

Hey Terra,

I have very high standards when it comes to the guys I go out with, but lately, I haven't had much luck meeting the kind of guys I'm interested in. My mom says that I shouldn't be so picky because "nobody's perfect." What do you think?

Where Is Love?

Dear Where Is Love,

I agree: nobody's perfect. But happiness doesn't come from lowering your standards. It's okay to be "picky" because *you* are the one who needs to be comfortable with your choice. If you're clear about which qualities matter to you, stick with them.

On the other hand, you might ask yourself if you're focusing more on looks than character traits. Are you having trouble meeting guys because you only want ones who fit very narrow standards of "good-looking"? Is there a chance that you keep changing your standards every time a new guy pays attention to you? If this is the case, your inner voice may be telling you you're not ready to have a boyfriend. Spend time thinking about what you really need. I wish you the best.

In friendship,
Terra

What makes a great girlfriend, anyway?

Hey Terra,

I look at the girls my friends go out with, and the guys say these girls are "great," but I don't see what's so great about them. They talk too much, and they're always complaining if my friends don't call them all the time and take them out every weekend. And these girls get really jealous when the guys talk to any other girl, even if it's just to say hi or to ask about homework. So, what makes a great girlfriend, anyway?

Just Wondering

Dear Just Wondering,

Each person has his/her own ideas about what makes another person "great." Maybe this is why the girls your friends think are cool don't really appeal to you. Ultimately, *you* are the only person who knows what matters most to you.

Think about the girls you've been attracted to. Are they at all similar? Do they share certain qualities or personality traits? Now think about your friends and what you like about them. Do you share common interests? Do they like you for who you are? You'll probably realize that the qualities you admire in your friends are some of the very same qualities you're looking for in a girlfriend. The more aware you are of what you want, the more likely you'll be to get what you need from a relationship—and to give something in return. Take care.

In friendship,
Terra

Where can I find a boyfriend who will stay?

Send

Hey Terra,

My problem isn't meeting guys or getting them to like me. It's finding one who will stick around for more than three weeks (that's my record for boyfriends). It's like I fall in love, everything's going great, and then the next thing I know it's over, and I don't even know what went wrong! I wish I had a boyfriend who would stay with me!

Stumped

Dear Stumped,

The most successful relationships include open communication about what matters most to the people involved (especially in the early stages of the relationship). If you talk openly from day one, you're more likely to handle problems as they come up, instead of realizing that something must have gone wrong after the relationship ends.

Loving involves learning. But if you don't get feedback, you'll never know what you've done to contribute to a breakup. The next time you're interested in a guy who likes you, talk honestly with him and see if he has the same values when it comes to communication. If he doesn't, you'll know right away that he isn't the guy for you. Good luck!

In friendship,
Terra

How come some girls like guys who treat them badly?

Hey Terra,

I'm a smart guy and a good musician. I'm also good-hearted and not at all bad looking. My problem is that the girls in my school seem to only be into going out with guys who treat them like total "crap." Is my problem that I respect women too much?

What's Up?

Dear What's Up,

You don't have a problem, but the girls you've been observing do (and that goes for their boyfriends, too)! Any girl who's attracted to a guy who treats her badly probably has low self-esteem. My guess is that this isn't the kind of girl you're looking for. Keep on treating girls with respect, which means as your equal. Someday, the kind of girl you're looking for will come into your life and appreciate what a great guy you are! I wish you well.

In friendship,
Terra

CHAPTER 3

Making Boyfriend/Girlfriend Relationships Work

When you're ready to venture into the boyfriend/girlfriend zone, the world becomes a place filled with romantic possibilities: "Did you see the way she looked at me?" "I wonder if he likes me." "Will anyone ever ask me out?" "Will this relationship last?" Your love interests may shift from day to day like changing kaleidoscope patterns. And once you're in a romantic relationship, you may have all sorts of new emotions—and questions! One of the main ones will probably be, "How do we make this relationship work?"

BUILDING HEALTHY RELATIONSHIPS

A healthy romantic relationship includes lots of elements, but here are the basic ones: *honesty, respect, trust,* and *open communication.* They're not listed in order of importance—they're all *equally* important. If you have all four ingredients, a relationship can grow in healthy ways. (By the way, these ingredients are necessary for *all* healthy relationships, including the ones you have with your friends, parents, teachers, and other people in your life. But for now, we're talking about boyfriends/girlfriends.)

What do healthy romantic relationships look like? Truthfully, they're not easy for outsiders to recognize. If you're on the outside looking in, you could be fooled by what you see. Some couples always act lovey-dovey around other people, but they may not be so loving when they're alone. Other couples are shy and don't reveal much about what's going on in their relationship. And still other couples, for whatever reason, act as if they don't care about (or even like) each other at all! This is why romantic relationships are such a mystery.

To find out if your relationship is healthy, be aware of how you and your bf/gf treat each other. Is there honesty, respect, trust, and open communication? Are these elements always there, or there most of the time, or never there at all? How do you feel when you're with your bf/gf? Happy? Proud? Safe? Or are you nervous about saying or doing the "wrong" thing? Do you talk openly about what's on your mind, or do you keep lots of secrets from each other? Understanding what a healthy relationship is can help you "fix" yours when it heads in an unhealthy direction.

Honesty

Honesty is the freedom to be who you are, without pretending. It means you speak from the heart and openly share your feelings and opinions. You're in an honest relationship when both of you can be "real" with each other when you're feeling happy or down, and whether you're alone or with others. In such a relationship, neither person wonders if the other is telling the truth, because it's *always* the truth.

Joe has a girlfriend, but last weekend he met another girl at the community center. The girl liked him right away and offered to give him her phone number. Joe liked her, too, but he told her that he already had a girlfriend and didn't take the phone number.

Does Joe's relationship have honesty? Yes. He was honest with the girl who wanted to give him her phone number, and more important, he was true to his girlfriend.

Healthy or **Unhealthy Sign?**

Alisha told her boyfriend that she couldn't go to the dance because her parents were going out for a romantic dinner, and she had to baby-sit. She knew that her parents were really going to see a divorce lawyer.

Does Alisha's relationship have honesty? No. She doesn't feel comfortable telling the truth about her family problems. Instead of sharing what's going on, she keeps her boyfriend in the dark about something that's really bothering her.

Telling lies is dishonest. People lie for lots of different reasons, such as:

- They want to protect themselves or hide something they've done. ("I didn't do it!")
- They want to protect someone's feelings. ("Your haircut looks great, so stop worrying about it.")
- They're trying to get what they want. ("I'm sixteen. Really!")
- They don't trust someone enough to tell the truth. ("I just don't feel like going, that's all.")

Some people think that lying solves problems, but it usually creates many more. Lying to your boyfriend/girlfriend puts distance between you, because when you lie, you then need to make sure that he/she doesn't find out the truth. And covering up your lies takes away from time the two of you could spend together being genuine. If you've ever been dishonest, you probably know that lying doesn't *help* a relationship. Instead, lying often causes confusion, guilt, and pain. Some people believe "a little deception" is good for a relationship. They're wrong!

To have a healthy relationship, you need to be honest with yourself and with the other person. If you do things you aren't comfortable discussing, the solution isn't to lie. Start listening to your inner voice (see pages 6–10 for how to do this), which helps you figure out the right choices to make. The more comfortable you are telling the truth, the more often you can do it!

I lied to my girlfriend, and I'm afraid she'll find out

Hey Terra,

I gave a necklace to a girl I used to go out with. She never wore it, and when we broke up, she gave it back to me. I have a new girlfriend now, and it was our one-month anniversary. I gave her the necklace. A friend of mine saw her wear it and said, "Isn't that the necklace you gave 'T'?" I quickly said, "No!" and tried to change the subject. My girlfriend wears the necklace all the time, so now I'm afraid my ex (who has a big mouth) is going to say something about it to her. Help, please!

In Big Trouble

Dear In Big Trouble,

I would suggest telling your girlfriend the truth before she finds out from your ex or someone else. You might say, "What I told you before about the necklace wasn't the truth. It *is* the same one I gave to 'T,' but she never wore it. It makes me happy to see you wearing it. It looks really nice on you, and I'm glad you like it. I'm very sorry that I lied to you, and I promise not to do it again."

My guess is that your girlfriend will appreciate your honesty and your promise to be truthful, so I don't think you'll be in too much trouble. Just make sure that you stick to the truth from now on! Good luck!

In friendship,
Terra

My boyfriend doesn't know that I'm part black

Hey Terra,

My dad is black, and my mom is white. I'm pretty light skinned and, at first, people who don't know me think I'm from another country. My parents love each other a lot, and they've always taught me and my sister that race doesn't matter as much as the kind of person you are. We recently moved, and my new school has very few black students. My new boyfriend is white, and he thinks I'm Iranian because that's what I told him. He'll probably never meet my parents, so there's no harm in that, is there?

Just Checking

Dear Just Checking,

I understand that you lied because you were afraid of rejection. Maybe you're thinking that your boyfriend wouldn't feel the same way about you if he found out you're biracial. But a romantic relationship (or any relationship for that matter) needs honesty. Tell your boyfriend the truth.

Your parents are right: a person's character is more important than skin color. Anyone worth calling a "friend" or "boyfriend/girlfriend" will accept you for *you*. If your race is hard for your boyfriend to accept, he's not the right guy for you.

Be proud of your parents and the fact that you're a part of each of them. Take care.

In friendship,
Terra

Cheating (dishonesty)

The most extreme form of dishonesty in a romantic relationship is cheating on each other. What you and your bf/gf consider cheating depends on the agreements you've made together. For example, if you've agreed not to date anyone else and one of you does, that's cheating. If you've agreed not to flirt with anyone else and one of you does, *that's* cheating. Being dishonest in this way shows a lack of respect for your romantic partner and the relationship, too. And doing something you know is wrong can make you lose respect for yourself.

If either person in a romantic relationship is unfaithful to the other, it's going to create problems. So why *do* people cheat, especially when it can be so hurtful to the person they care about? People cheat for lots of reasons, but mostly because they don't have the maturity or integrity to do the right thing in spite of what they're feeling, physically and emotionally.

The world is filled with attractive people, and there's nothing wrong with noticing them. Sometimes it's confusing when you feel turned on by someone who you aren't dating. Does it mean you don't like or love your bf/gf anymore? Not necessarily. Just because you *feel* attracted to someone else doesn't mean you have to *do* anything about it. (Review the differences between feelings of love and lust on pages 41–47.)

If you've never cheated before but you're considering it, stop and ask yourself these questions:

- Am I happy in my current relationship? Why or why not?
- If I cheat, how will my boyfriend/girlfriend feel when he/she finds out?
- If I'm unfaithful, how will I feel about myself?
- How would I feel if someone did this to me?
- How will other people feel about me if they find out I cheated?
- Do I want to be known as a cheater?

If you *have* broken your agreements by seeing other people and you want to save the relationship, ask yourself these questions:

• Why did I betray my boyfriend/girlfriend? Maybe you're not sure why you did it, but if you look deeply enough, you can find the reason. Were you trying to get back at your bf/gf for some past hurt? Were you proving to yourself that you're attractive to other people? Were you under the influence of alcohol or another drug at the time? Think about the reasons behind your choice.

• Did I cheat to get out of my relationship? Sometimes, without really understanding why, people sabotage or wreck their relationships. Cheating as a "shortcut" to breaking up isn't honest, and hurting your bf/gf is *never* a solution. Instead, talk about your feelings, even if it feels uncomfortable to do so.

• **What did I feel when I was with the other person that I don't feel with my boyfriend/girlfriend?** Sometimes there's something important missing in a relationship. If you know what it is but you don't talk to your bf/gf about it, you'll probably end up going outside of the relationship to find it. That's not honest or respectful. Take your concerns about the relationship directly to the person involved and try to resolve the issues that are troubling you. That's how relationships grow.

• **How will I make up for the hurt I've caused?** To repair the broken trust in your relationship, apologize and promise that you won't cheat anymore. If your bf/gf decides to trust you, make sure that you don't betray that trust again.

If cheating caused your relationship to end, forgive yourself. From now on, think more carefully about your decisions, and use this experience as an opportunity to understand yourself and all your relationships a little better. Don't give up on yourself!

Why do I keep cheating on my girlfriend?

Hey Terra,

I have a great girlfriend, but I cheat on her a lot. I don't know why I keep hurting her like this. Do you have any ideas?

Feeling Bad

Dear Feeling Bad,

You're already aware of how hurtful and dishonest your behavior is, and that's the first step. Now you need to understand why you continue to cheat. What message are you sending your girlfriend by cheating? Can you tell her in words, instead of through negative actions, what's on your mind? You may need help figuring out why you've repeatedly betrayed your girlfriend. Talk to your school counselor or another adult you respect and trust.

Until you know what's *really* going on, it may be best to end this relationship, rather than keep hurting your girlfriend. She doesn't deserve this treatment (no one does). Promise yourself that you'll only get involved with someone when you're ready to have a relationship based on honesty, respect, trust, and open communication. I wish you well.

In friendship,
Terra

Is he cheating or not?

Hey Terra,

My boyfriend used to be so in love with me, and I felt the same way. I still love him as much (maybe more), but he's really changed. He never seems to want to spend time with me, and when I call him, he's never there. Then when I ask him where he was, he gets all mad. I'm careful not to push him because I don't want him to break up with me. Yesterday, his friend asked me if I'd break up with my boyfriend if I found out he was cheating on me. I didn't answer, but it sure made me wonder why he asked me that. What should I do?

Confused

Dear Confused,

If it looks like cheating and smells like cheating, it probably *is* cheating. That might explain your boyfriend's behavior. If he feels guilty about the betrayal, he may be putting distance between you (because it's easier than telling you the truth).

When you say you're careful not to push him, do you mean that you don't ask him what's going on? He needs to know how you feel about the way he's been treating you. I hope that you can share your feelings honestly. If not, this relationship isn't healthy. You deserve better, and you deserve the truth!

In friendship,
Terra

I cheated on my jealous boyfriend

Hey Terra,

My boyfriend and I have been together for seven months. He's very jealous and accuses me of cheating on him all the time, which I'd never done until last weekend. At a camp reunion, I was with a guy who I was just friends with over the summer. We ended up having sex, and now I feel guilty. The thing is, I don't even really care about the guy I slept with, though he likes me a lot. I think that if my boyfriend wasn't always accusing me of cheating, I probably wouldn't have done it. What now?

Uh-oh

Dear Uh-oh,

Sounds like you're making excuses for your behavior. Your boyfriend may act jealous, but this doesn't give you the right to cheat on him. Own up to the fact that *you* chose to be disloyal, and then figure out why you did it. Once you know, you can start repairing the damage.

Your boyfriend's jealousy may be a sign that he's insecure and controlling. Is it possible that you cheated to get out of the relationship? Next time, be honest with someone you're in a relationship with *and* be true to yourself.

And what about the guy you had sex with? Take some time to think about his feelings. Does he think you two are a couple now? I hope you'll take a hard look at the situation and do what you can to fix it. Have courage and tell the guy you had sex with that you made a mistake.

The good news is that every experience can be a learning opportunity. Take what you learned from this difficult situation and use it to make honest and honorable choices in the future. Good luck!

In friendship,
Terra

Respect

Some people think that they should only respect someone who has a "higher status" than they do. It's true that people in positions of authority often command great respect. (To find out more about authority figures and how you can improve your relationships with them, read Chapter 8, "Dealing with Authority Figures.") While it's an excellent idea to treat authority figures with respect, *real* respect has nothing to do with one person being above someone else. In fact, in the healthiest relationships, both people feel equal and treat each other respectfully.

To respect someone means you *value* that person. Maybe you value the person for his/her personality, character traits, or other qualities. Or maybe it's because of a certain choice the person has made or the way he/she treats others. When you respect someone, you treat that person in the same way *you* would like to be treated—with kindness, honesty, and consideration.

 Brad and his girlfriend, Carla, are talking with some friends about a movie they've just seen. Brad thinks the starring actress was "hot," and Carla says the actress had an "awful voice." Brad laughs and announces, "You should talk! You can't sing to save your life."

Was Brad showing respect for Carla? Not at all. When Brad made fun of Carla's voice, he embarrassed her in front of her friends. When someone treats you with respect, that person doesn't put you down publicly or privately.

 Danielle just found out that her favorite aunt is a lesbian. She tells her boyfriend, LeRoy, how confused she is but asks him not to tell anyone else about the situation. Later, a friend asks LeRoy what's going on with Danielle. He replies, "She doesn't want to talk about it, so give her a chance to work it out on her own. If she wants to talk, we'll be there for her."

Did LeRoy show respect for Danielle? Absolutely. He didn't tell anyone about the situation, at her request. He respected her need for privacy, understanding that she preferred to be alone with her thoughts and feelings.

In relationships that lack respect, one person may feel in control of the other (and may even think that he/she has the "right" to put down, insult, or embarrass the other person). A serious lack of respect in a relationship can lead to verbal, emotional, physical, or sexual abuse. For more information about the warning signs of an abusive relationship, see pages 106–113. For now, remember that you have every right to be treated with consideration. It's better to be single than to be in a relationship in which you're not being treated with respect.

My boyfriend calls me names   Send

Hey Terra,

My boyfriend and I get along well, except when we're around his friends. That's the only time he's really rude to me, calling me names like "Chunk" and "Dumbo." I've told him I don't appreciate it, and he says he's just joking and that I'm too sensitive. Am I?

Not Laughing

Dear Not Laughing,

What your boyfriend is doing isn't funny, so don't accept his excuse that it's only a "joke." Because he acts this way when his friends are around, he probably thinks his behavior makes him look cooler in their eyes. All it really does is make him look like he doesn't know how to treat a girlfriend with respect!

Tell him that you won't put up with his name-calling anymore (joke or no joke). To make sure he gets the message this time, you might say, "If you can't treat me with respect when your friends are around, I don't want to continue this relationship." If things don't improve, keep your promise and break up with him. You're better off without someone who brings you down. I wish you well.

In friendship,
Terra

My girlfriend is always late

Hey Terra,

This may not seem like a major problem compared to some letters you get, but my girlfriend always keeps me waiting whenever I pick her up to go somewhere, and it bothers me. I'm not just talking about a minute or two, but more like twenty or thirty minutes, every single time. Because of that, we always miss the beginning of movies. I really love everything else about her, and I don't want to break up with her, but I have to admit that when I'm sitting on the couch waiting, I get annoyed. What can I do to make her be ready on time?

Always Waiting

Dear Always Waiting,

If you haven't already told your girlfriend how you feel, do it now. Her behavior shows a lack of respect for you and your time, and respect is an essential part of a healthy relationship.

Some people seem to be chronically late, but they can learn to better handle their schedules. If your girlfriend is willing to change, work with her. For example, if you're going to a movie that starts at 8:00 and it takes ten minutes to get from her house to the theater, tell her you'll be at her house at 7:15. Call before you leave your house to give her fair warning. She should be ready to go when you arrive.

The most important thing to do is to tell her that you want to be treated with respect. Let her know that when she's constantly late, you feel like you aren't important to her. If your girlfriend isn't willing to be on time for you, you have a decision to make: you can leave the relationship, or you can stay with her and continue to be irritated when she's late. Another choice is to accept that she won't ever be ready on time, and then bring a book so you'll have something to do while waiting. It's up to you to decide! I wish you the best.

In friendship,
Terra

Trust

Trust means knowing that your boyfriend/girlfriend has your well-being in mind. Mutual trust is when your bf/gf feels the same way. When you both act with honesty and treat each other with respect, you know you can count on each other. Trust is the foundation of a healthy relationship because it allows you to feel at ease and be certain that your boyfriend/girlfriend won't suddenly turn against you. When you trust someone and the person is trustworthy (deserving of your trust), there's no need for jealousy or doubt. You're both free to be yourselves, which brings out the best in each of you.

Manuel has several close friends who are girls. His girl-friend doesn't like him hanging out with them. She says a good boyfriend should spend his free time with his girlfriend.

Is there trust in this relationship? No. Manuel's girlfriend seems to have trouble trusting him. She feels the need to control him and how he spends his time. A relationship that lacks trust isn't growing in a healthy way.

Andrea heard through a mutual friend that her boyfriend, Tony, asked out another girl. This friend told Andrea to break up with Tony before he broke up with her. She didn't believe the rumor and talked to Tony. She found out that none of it was true—he hadn't asked any other girl out.

Is there trust in this relationship? Yes. Andrea trusts that Tony won't betray her. She doesn't allow herself to jump to conclusions about rumors. Instead, she talks to Tony before reacting and assuming, and her trust is confirmed. This is a healthy sign.

I don't know if I trust my girlfriend

Send

Hey Terra,

My girlfriend and I have been together for four months. She had this other boyfriend for about a year, and he still calls her. I know this because my girlfriend's sister told me, but when I asked my girlfriend, she said he doesn't call her. But then a few days ago, she said he does. I asked her if she still loves him, and she gave me a funny look and said, "We're just friends." I really want to believe her, but some of my friends knew her when she was going out with this other guy and they say the two of them were a hot couple. So, here's my problem: can I trust my girlfriend when she says she loves me? I really love her so I want to believe her, but something inside of me says she's lying.

Am I the One?

Dear Am I the One,

Your girlfriend might be hiding something from you, which could explain why she changed her story about the phone calls. But, in fairness, are you making it safe for her to talk to you honestly? Ask yourself these questions: How would you feel if she had a friendship with her ex? Would that be okay? And, if so, have you told her you'd accept it? My suggestion is that you and your girlfriend have a conversation about the importance of honesty and trust. Can you both agree to be more open with each other? Healthy relationships need trust to work. Good luck!

In friendship,
Terra

Jealousy (lack of trust)

Jealousy is a powerful emotion that you feel in your head and body. Your chest may tighten up, your stomach may feel weird, and you may be so out of control emotionally that you can't even think straight. When you feel jealous, you believe someone else has something you want. For example, you might feel jealous of someone who gets new clothes, the lead in the school play, an A on a test, or praise from a teacher.

In a romantic relationship, you might feel jealous if someone gets attention from your boyfriend/girlfriend. You may also feel threatened, hurt, confused, angry, and less loved than you were before. It doesn't make a lot of sense when you really think about it, but it's still the way you feel.

People in trusting and healthy relationships aren't jealous when their bf/gf spends time with others. If you're involved with someone right now, ask yourself how you feel when he/she is out with friends. Are you worried he/she is cheating or will find someone to replace you? Do you imagine that your bf/gf is having more fun with friends than he/she ever does with you? If you feel this way, your relationship lacks trust. Maybe you've been disappointed and betrayed often in your life, which can make it hard for you to trust other people. But unless you and your bf/gf learn to trust each other, jealousy is bound to occur.

What's the best way to handle jealousy? *By using your mind and not your emotions.* Often, when people are jealous, they've totally misinterpreted a situation. What they *thought* was going on wasn't happening. They may make assumptions, accept a rumor as the truth, or believe the worst of someone. In other words, they stop thinking straight and let their emotions take over. To stay in control:

1. Don't jump to conclusions.
2. Take some time to breathe deeply and let yourself calm down.
3. Talk to yourself about what's going on. Is there another explanation for what you saw or heard?
4. Once you're feeling calm and level-headed, talk with your boyfriend/girlfriend so you can resolve things.

If you think that your bf/gf flirted with someone else, stop and think before acting on your emotions. Do you two have an agreement not to flirt with others? If you don't, make one. If you *do* have this type of agreement, avoid jumping to conclusions about his/her behavior. Check out the facts first. What exactly happened, and did you see it with your own eyes? Are you hearing the information from someone you trust and who has your best interests at heart? Have you asked your bf/gf about it? By seeking out the truth, you might save yourself from a major meltdown. You'll also get the satisfaction of knowing you've handled a situation maturely.

But what if your jealousy *is* justified? Suppose your boyfriend/girlfriend really is flirting (or worse)? It's time for open communication and for you to make decisions about what you want and *don't* want out of this relationship. Read pages 229–237 in Chapter 9, "Conflict Resolution Tool Kit," which can help you find healthy ways to confront problems.

My boyfriend gets mad if I talk to other guys

Hey Terra,

My boyfriend gets really jealous whenever I talk to another guy. I've never cheated on him or anything. It's just that I'm friendly, and I have lots of guy friends. I told my boyfriend he has nothing to be jealous about, but he still questions me about everything. Like when he calls me and the line is busy he'll say, "Who were you just talking to?" I don't like the way he's acting, but I don't know what to do. My friends say I should be happy because his behavior shows he loves me a lot. I'm not so sure. What do you think?

Joe's Girl

Dear Joe's Girl,

You have every right to talk to other people, male or female, face-to-face or on the phone. Only an insecure boyfriend would feel threatened by his girlfriend's guy friends. You aren't his property! You're a free and independent young woman.

Tell your boyfriend how you feel when he acts jealous. Your words can help him understand that his behavior creates distance, not closeness. He needs to trust you in the same way that you need to trust him. Ask him to stop questioning you about conversations you have with others. When you talk, give him a chance to express his concerns and feelings. A relationship without trust and open communication doesn't have much of a future. I wish you both the best.

In friendship,
Terra

My boyfriend has two girlfriends!

Hey Terra,

Should I tell my boyfriend that I know he's got another girlfriend who goes to a different school? I know it's true because a really good friend of mine goes to that school and has seen my boyfriend and this girl kissing at basketball games and school dances.

Miserable

Dear Miserable,

Did you and your boyfriend make an agreement not to date other people? If not, it's time to talk about whether you both want this kind of relationship. If you already *do* have this type of agreement, he's betrayed your trust, and he owes you an apology. Tell your boyfriend what you've heard and how you feel, so you can find out how much he values your relationship. If he likes things the way they are (and you don't), it's up to you to decide whether you're willing to continue going out with him even though he's seeing someone else. Thanks for writing.

In friendship,
Terra

Communication

Besides respect and trust, healthy relationships require open communication. That means you and your boyfriend/girlfriend talk freely—there aren't "off-limits" subjects between you—and you can express your feelings without judgment. Using open communication, the two of you can learn about each other on a very personal level and come to understand each other more deeply.

Jackie and Shawn have an agreement not to get involved romantically with other people. Jackie went to a party without Shawn and kissed someone else. She didn't tell Shawn because she didn't want to hurt his feelings. Shawn heard about the kiss but didn't ask Jackie about it, because he was afraid it might be true.

Does this relationship have open communication? No. If it did, Jackie would have talked to Shawn about what she did and why. As for Shawn, he knows something's not right, but unless he talks openly with Jackie, the problem can't be fixed.

Whenever Kevin is in a bad mood and his girlfriend, Janna, asks him what's wrong, he snaps, "I don't want to talk about it." Janna is frustrated that Kevin won't share his feelings with her.

Is there open communication here? Not really. While Janna might understand that everyone needs some private time, it's frustrating for her to feel so shut out. If Kevin doesn't learn to open up, this relationship probably won't grow in healthy ways. With open communication, Kevin could learn to talk about his feelings, and Janna could give him the support he needs.

Most problems in romantic relationships result from poor communication or none at all. It's easy to *say* you're going to communicate better, but doing so is another thing altogether. Many people simply aren't comfortable talking about their feelings—even with family members. To open up may feel a bit strange, and you may not know exactly how to express yourself. So how can you improve your communication with your boyfriend/girlfriend?

Recognizing that you need open communication is an excellent place to start. Understanding how poor communication creates problems is also important. Watch for the warning signs of a communication breakdown—do you grow apart, fight more, or feel tempted to cheat or break up? Share what you're feeling, even if it seems weird or embarrassing at first. To find out what to say and how to listen when you're working on a relationship problem, check out Chapter 9, "Conflict Resolution Tool Kit," on pages 229–237.

I wish my girlfriend talked to me more

Hey Terra,

My girlfriend is really smart, but when we're alone she doesn't talk all that much. Most of the time, I feel like I'm doing all the talking. Why doesn't she talk more?

Talker

Dear Talker,

Some people are naturally shy and prefer listening to talking. Maybe you can draw your girlfriend into a conversation by asking her questions about herself, her feelings, and her interests.

If you've tried this and it hasn't worked, tell her how you feel and what you need. You might say, "I feel like I do all the talking in our relationship. I feel pressured to keep the conversation going. I'd like it if you would open up and talk more, because I'd like to get to know you better." I hope this helps!

In friendship,
Terra

How come boys don't talk about their feelings?

Hey Terra,

We girls all agree that it's a lot easier for us to talk about our feelings than it is for guys to talk about theirs. Why is that?

Girls Who'll Say Anything

Dear Girls Who'll Say Anything,

It may seem as though only boys have a hard time expressing feelings, but some girls find this to be a challenge, too. In our society, males are taught that "boys don't cry" and showing "tenderhearted" emotions like sadness isn't considered masculine. In the same way, females are taught that showing anger isn't feminine. These mistaken beliefs hold everyone back! Men and women, boys and girls *all* benefit from expressing emotions honestly.

As humans, we experience many emotions every day—embarrassment, sadness, love, happiness, shyness, insecurity, anger, compassion, frustration, and so on. When we don't express our feelings, we lose touch with them and part of what makes us fully human.

If you want the guys in your life to talk more openly about their feelings, tell them so. You might say, "It helps me feel close to you when I know what's going on with you. You're such a great listener when I have problems, and I want to be there for you in the same way." Don't pressure or lay guilt trips on your boyfriends over this issue. Words like, "What's wrong with you? Why don't you ever talk about your feelings? Don't you trust me?!" never help.

Talking about feelings is scary for some people. Be patient and continue being open yourself—this may encourage your boyfriends to do the same. Also, if you treat your boyfriends with respect and really listen to what they have to say, they'll feel safer sharing their feelings. Be persistent!

In friendship,
Terra

REDEFINING RELATIONSHIPS

People change and so do their needs and their relationships. Sometimes new feelings lead to the change. Other times, relationships shift when people move on. Life presents changes and challenges all the time. You may not have control over what happens, but you always have *choices* about how you handle things.

"Redefining" a relationship may mean becoming romantically involved with someone who was previously just a friend, or could mean breaking up with a romantic partner. Relationship changes may force the people involved to be more honest and trusting, to treat each other with more respect, and to communicate more openly. So don't be afraid of change. Use it as a chance to figure out what you really want and need right now. Then make sure you communicate this.

From nearby to long distance

Suppose you and your boyfriend/girlfriend attend the same school. You even share many of the same classes. On weekends, it's no problem seeing each other because you live relatively close by. Now suppose that one of you moves away. What happens? The relationship is in for some definite changes.

If your bf/gf no longer lives near enough for you to see each other even once a month without serious planning, it doesn't matter whether the distance is 100 miles or 1,000 miles. This kind of relationship is difficult! Separation from someone you love can be emotionally—and even physically—painful.

Many teens write to ask me if a long-distance relationship can last. To be honest, the odds aren't great. You and your boyfriend/girlfriend are changing so much from day to day, and if you aren't around each other often, it's only natural to drift apart. This doesn't mean it's *impossible* for your relationship to last, but the physical distance between you makes staying together more difficult.

The best way to handle the separation (and the sadness and longing that comes with it) is to stay close in other ways. You can keep up with each other's lives by communicating often. Email makes this easy, but you can also make phone calls, write letters, and exchange photos, audiotapes, poetry, and art. Being creative with how you keep in touch will help you feel emotionally closer to the person, even if he/she is physically very far away.

When you're separated from your boyfriend/girlfriend, it's important to stay involved in your own activities. Being "a million miles away" in your head and your heart is a challenge, but daydreaming endlessly won't help. If you put your life on hold until you're with the one you love, your relationships with your friends and family will suffer. You have to be where you are, or you're nowhere at all. Use your "single" time to focus on activities, school, hobbies, friends, or whatever your interests are. Enjoy life!

My girlfriend lives in another part of the state

Hey Terra,

My girlfriend is really great, but now she lives in another part of the state and we don't see each other much (like hardly ever). I love her, but there's this girl I just recently met who goes to my school and we get along great, too. I think I love them both, and they both say they love me. You see the problem?

Caught in the Middle

Dear Caught in the Middle,

A long-distance relationship is obviously different than a "nearby" one. When there's distance between you, it's tough to stay close. (That's the downside.) But not being able to see each other has an "up" side, too. It gives both of you the freedom to do other things, such as going out with friends. With a girlfriend who lives nearby, on the other hand, you might want to go out with her as much as possible. As a result, you both may lose some independence.

You have a decision to make: do you want to stick with the long-distance relationship and see where it goes? Or do you want to pursue the girl who's nearby? Or do you want to date both, which may or may not be acceptable to them?

Before you get further involved with the local girl, tell your girlfriend what's going on. Explain how you're feeling about the relationship, the distance, and the fact that you have feelings for someone else. Have this conversation soon, because it sounds as though you have two girls who think they're the only one, and that's one girl too many (unless both girls are okay sharing you). Best of luck!

In friendship,
Terra

How can our relationship last when my boyfriend is away?

Hey Terra,

I'm seventeen, and I'm in love with my boyfriend who's so sweet and caring. Other relationships never lasted because the guys were jerks and also because I was too immature to know what I really wanted. Now I know, and I feel so lucky to have found the right guy. The problem is this: my boyfriend is transferring out of state to a large university, and I have another year of high school. I wonder if the relationship can last while he's away. I can't bear to think about what my life will be like without him. Is there anything I can do to make sure we're always in love the way we are now?

Juliet

Dear Juliet,

It's wonderful to find someone who's sweet and caring. I'm sure the thought of losing that closeness is difficult. But your boyfriend needs to pursue his education and his dreams, and you have a life to live where you are. I know you're looking for definite answers, but some things in life just have to happen as they happen.

There are no guarantees that your love will last. The best I can suggest is that you and your boyfriend communicate openly and frequently about what's going on and how you're feeling, now and when you're apart. The good news is that with chat rooms, instant messaging, and email, it's easier than ever to keep the channels of communication open. And regular mail is still a fun way to keep in touch. Enjoy your last year of high school and know that your relationship will work out exactly the way it's supposed to. Also, know that you can enjoy your life with or without a boyfriend. Thanks for writing.

In friendship,
Terra

Friends or something more?

When someone you really like says, "I just want to be friends," it can be hard to take, especially when you see that person being romantic with someone else. You may be hurting, but you're not helpless. You *always* have choices for handling any situation. Ask yourself these questions:

• **Is a friendship better than nothing?** It might be, if you like the person and can put aside your romantic feelings and enjoy the friendship. On the other hand, you may have trouble shelving your emotions. In this case, it may be wiser to choose *not* to be friends for now.

• **Can I really be a good friend?** You may find that you can't be with the person without wishing the relationship were more than it is. If so, maybe you *can't* be a good friend until your romantic feelings subside. In that case, saying "no thanks" is a healthy decision.

Friendships with people you like more than "just friends" *can* work. If, in your heart, the friendship feels right, this could be a great opportunity to learn about yourself and what it means to be a true friend. Remember, many successful romantic relationships start out as friendships. This may not happen in your case . . . but then again, it might!

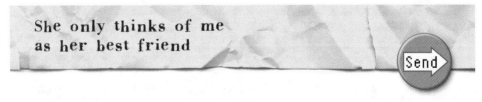

She only thinks of me as her best friend

Send

Hey Terra,

I already know what I want in a girlfriend. I've even met her! The problem is she just thinks of me as her best friend. She's a great girl, and if her stupid boyfriend wasn't around making her life so miserable by cheating on her, she might notice that I have feelings for her that are way more serious than just friendship. She always asks for my advice, but what should I tell her to get her to wake up and see that the guy who loves her most is standing right here?!

Just J.J.'s Friend

Dear Just J.J.'s Friend,

Have you told your friend how you really feel about her? You have some choices for handling this situation:

1. Tell her that you like her as more than a friend. She may have no idea about your true feelings. If she did, hers might change! If her feelings for you stay the same, at least you've been honest.

2. Don't tell her about your romantic feelings. Simply continue being her best friend. She obviously likes you, trusts you, and appreciates your friendship. That's a good thing, because friendship counts for a lot.

3. Stop being her friend. If it's too painful for you to be in this friendship, especially when she asks for advice about her boyfriend, give yourself some time away from her.

If she breaks up with her boyfriend and you're still interested in her romantically, ask her out. Once you do, she may be able to see you in a whole new light. Good luck!

In friendship,
Terra

I went out with my best friend, but it didn't work out

Hey Terra,

Maybe it was a mistake, but my best guy friend and I went out for about three weeks, and then it just wasn't working so we broke up. We decided it was better to be best friends instead. Well, he was actually the one who decided. He wasn't interested in me romantically. I went along with it, but I still really like him in a romantic way, although he doesn't know that. Now the friendship doesn't feel the same as it did before. How long will it take to get back to the way it was?

Friends Again

Dear Friends Again,

You took the plunge and tried to go from a friendship to a romantic relationship. As you've discovered, it can be a challenge to switch gears this way!

It doesn't sound as if you're ready to be just friends again. To give the relationship a little breathing room, spend time with people you're totally comfortable with and try to meet some new friends. When your feelings for this guy aren't so intense, see if you can go back to being friends again. I hope things work out!

In friendship,
Terra

Should I tell her how I feel?

Send

Hey Terra,

Lately, I've had feelings for a girl I've been friends with since fourth grade. We've always gotten along really well. Even when other kids in the class teased us about liking each other, it never spoiled our friendship. So now I'm thinking I really *do* like her as more than a friend. Should I tell her how I feel? If I do, how can I tell her without being scared that she'll laugh or something?

Freaked

Dear Freaked,

Have you ever heard the expression "Nothing ventured, nothing gained"? It means that if you don't enter the contest, you can't possibly win. If you like this girl as more than just a friend, tell her. It's scary to express your true feelings, but it gets easier with practice. Rehearse what you want to say on your own or have another friend play the role of the girl. When you feel confident, arrange a time to talk and tell her the truth. The worst that can happen is that she may be embarrassed and surprised. More likely, the two of you will have a heartfelt talk that will help you get to know each other even better than before. Good luck!

In friendship,
Terra

Will he ever kiss me?

Hey Terra,

My boyfriend and I started out as friends, and then about a month ago we started going out. This is my first boyfriend, and I'm his first girlfriend. We're only in seventh grade, and he's on the shy side, but it's been two weeks already and he hasn't even held my hand! I want something romantic to happen between us. Do you think I should make the first move?

Waitin'

Dear Waitin',

While you seem to have successfully made the emotional shift from friends to something more, it sounds like your boyfriend isn't quite ready to get physical. Be patient—you haven't been going out very long. Holding hands will come in time. Usually, holding hands, hugging, and kissing takes a relationship to the next level, and these things happen when the time is right. Rushing into the physical stuff can be a mistake, especially if the other person isn't ready.

To get a little more intimate, you might hold his hand and see how he responds. If he likes it, fine, but if it makes him uncomfortable, respect that. The important thing is that the two of you enjoy being together and treat each other with respect. Take care.

In friendship,
Terra

CHAPTER 4

Sex, Unhealthy Romantic Relationships, and Good-byes

All *healthy* relationships grow in the direction of greater trust, more honesty, deeper respect, and more open communication. Romantic relationships also grow in yet another dimension. If you have a boyfriend/girlfriend, you may want to become closer to that person physically as well as emotionally, and you may be struggling with the confusing question, "How far should we go?"

When you're a teen, your body experiences hormone surges, physical changes, and an awakening of sexual feelings. Combine those changes and emotions with exposure to explicit song lyrics and sensual images on TV, in movies, and in magazines, add a dose of peer pressure from friends who may push you to become sexually active, and you may be wondering, "Should I be having sex? Is it right or wrong? What's right for me? What will happen if I have sex?"

Sex is a complicated issue—for adults as well as teens. This is because being sexually active involves deep emotional feelings and potentially life-changing physical risks. Sex also changes relationships and not always for the better (despite what the media images portray). *Before* you get too intimate, consider how sex might affect your feelings about yourself and your boyfriend/girlfriend and what the physical consequences might be.

Regardless of sexual activity, romances during the teen years are often short-lived. For this reason, it's important to recognize the warning signs of a relationship that's in trouble. When it's clear that you and your boyfriend/girlfriend want different things, you need to know how to say good-bye respectfully and move on with your life.

GETTING CLOSER PHYSICALLY

We're all physical, intellectual, and emotional beings. Identifying the different needs of the body, mind, and heart helps us, as humans, understand how we relate to one another. When we talk and exchange ideas, we connect with people intellectually—mind to mind. When we share our feelings and experiences, we connect emotionally—heart to heart. When we dance or play team sports we connect (and sometimes collide) physically—body to body.

But there's another kind of touching, *expressive touching*, which allows us to connect physically as well as intellectually and emotionally. Some examples of expressive touching are a handshake, a pat on the back, a hug, or a caress. These touches, along with our words and facial expressions, allow us to connect to people with caring and respect.

If you think back to your early relationship with your parents or other care-givers, or if you observe families in public places, you'll see many ways that parents use expressive touching to show their children how they feel. Children are carried, hugged, kissed, cuddled, or lifted up onto a lap. Parents hold their kids' hands, tousle their hair, or put an arm around their shoulders. All of these gestures say, "I love you. I'm here to comfort you and keep you safe."

As a preteen or teen, you may grow away from your parents emotionally and focus more on defining yourself as an individual. But as a human being, you don't outgrow your need to be touched. Wanting to touch and be touched is a basic human need. While you may not have the same physical closeness you once had with your mom or dad, you may have found it in other relationships. Friends, for example, often share feelings through hugs. The range of emotions a hug expresses could be everything from "We won!" to "I'm here for you" to "Great to see you."

Because of the romantic aspect of a boyfriend/girlfriend relationship, expressive touching takes on a whole new meaning, but it doesn't have to include sex. For example, holding hands is a way of connecting physically; it may also be a first step in acknowledging to each other, and your friends, that you're a couple. Another way to express intimacy, affection, and closeness is through hugging. Giving your romantic partner a hug (bringing him/her close to your heart) definitely allows you to feel closer emotionally.

Just as there are all kinds of hugs, there are also all kinds of kisses. You can kiss someone as a way to say hello or thank you. You can kiss a friend to show you care or to say, "I love you." A romantic kiss, though, is a very personal and intimate expression between two people.

Where does sex fit in with hugging and kissing? First, let's talk about the word "sex" because it can mean different things. On a purely physical level, sex is when certain body parts of one person come in contact with certain body parts of another person. In the simplest terms, these behaviors are *sexual activities,* sometimes referred to as "messing around." Obviously, all sexual behaviors (including touching of breasts or other body parts) aren't equal, but they all have a sexual intention. The most invasive sexual activity is *sexual intercourse,* or sexual contact that involves the genitals.

What's the big deal about sex in general and sexual intercourse in particular? *There are many risks involved.* Some of these risks are physical, while some are emotional.

SEX AND PHYSICAL RISKS

At this point in your life, you've probably learned a lot about sex through health classes, talking with parents or friends, reading about it, or even experimenting. But do you have enough information to make healthy decisions about it for yourself? Although, on some level, the physical act may seem simple, sex is complicated. Often, you hear different things about sex from different people— things that may or may not be true. This section covers the basics of the physical risks of sex. If you want more information, see the "Where to Turn" resources on page 100, and talk to an adult you respect and trust. (It's important to go to an adult because your friends, even though they mean well, may not have the most accurate information about sex.)

Pregnancy

If you engage in sexual activities, which may or may not include sexual intercourse, and you and your partner aren't using a condom or other form of *contraception* (birth control), you expose yourself to the possibility of pregnancy. Whether you're a guy or girl, you're at risk: as a girl, you can become pregnant; as a guy, you have responsibilities if your partner gets pregnant.

Can you get pregnant if you're not actually having sexual intercourse? Yes, and if you've heard otherwise, you've heard wrong! Anytime a guy's semen gets near a girl's vagina, there's a chance that sperm can enter the vagina, fertilize an egg, and cause a pregnancy. If you and your partner are using a condom, there's still a chance (one in eight) that the condom will break, slip, or otherwise fail to protect against pregnancy. The only 100 percent safe and effective method of protection against pregnancy is *abstinence*, which means not being sexually active.

Bottom line: You and your boyfriend/girlfriend are most likely *not* ready to deal with a pregnancy. That's why you need to think about the risks *before* you decide to have sex. One million American teen girls become pregnant each year, and one million teen boys are faced with fatherhood.

Sexually transmitted diseases (STDs)

If you engage in sexual activities and you and your partner aren't using a condom, you may be exposing yourself to sexually transmitted diseases. STDs are carried from person to person through sexual contact. Two very serious STDs are herpes and HIV.

• **Herpes:** Caused by a virus called HSV (herpes simplex virus), herpes is transmitted by unprotected sexual contact (vaginal, oral, or anal) with someone who has herpes. The herpes virus causes painful blisters that break into open sores. These sores may go away in five to twenty-one days, but the virus stays with you forever (there's no cure) and may be transmitted to other people. You may not know if someone has herpes because the sores aren't there all the time. Don't take chances.

- **HIV:** Human immunodeficiency virus (HIV) can cause AIDS (acquired immune deficiency syndrome), a life-threatening disease. AIDS hinders the body's ability to fight infections—it's the last stage of HIV infection and can kill you. HIV is transmitted in several ways, including unprotected sexual contact (vaginal, oral, or anal) with someone who has HIV; blood-to-blood contact with someone infected with HIV (this may occur when sharing unsterile needles during intravenous drug use); and through the breast milk of a nursing mother.

As with pregnancy, the only 100 percent safe and effective method of protection against STDs is abstinence.

In addition to herpes and HIV, there are dozens of other STDs that can have negative effects on your health. Unprotected sex puts you at high risk for getting them. Three million American teens are infected *each year*. Don't become one of them.

Did we have sex?   Send

Hey Terra,

My guy friend and I were just messing around, like we do sometimes. He had just taken a shower and I let him go inside me, only part way, one time. That wasn't really the same as having sex, was it?

Virgin

Dear Virgin,

Any penis-to-vagina contact is sex. And every time a guy puts his penis in your vagina (without a condom), you're at risk for pregnancy and sexually transmitted diseases (STDs). Sometimes teens think it's okay to have sex if a guy's penis is clean (you mentioned he had just taken a shower). Even if he scrubbed with antibacterial soap, and even if he's inside you for only a moment, you can still get pregnant or he can give you an infection, whether or not he ejaculates. In fact, you should take a pregnancy test to find out if you're pregnant and see a doctor to be tested for STDs.

I know this all may be a bit scary to hear, but what you and your friend are doing is very risky, and I hope you stop. I wish you well.

In friendship,
Terra

What is this rash?

Hey Terra,

My boyfriend and I were fooling around two weekends ago. We always use a condom, but this time we didn't. Nothing much happened, but well . . . a little bit happened. Now I have this weird rash on the inside part of my thigh, and it's right where he was touching me. I'm worried I might have an infection or something. How can I tell?

Itchy and Worried

Dear Itchy and Worried,

Whenever people get sexual without using protection, there's always a risk of pregnancy and sexually transmitted diseases (STDs). The only way you're going to be able to tell whether the rash is, in fact, an STD is to have it checked out by a doctor. I suggest you do that right away. Take care of yourself!

In friendship,
Terra

My girlfriend is pregnant!

Hey Terra,

My girlfriend and I have a big problem. She just took a home pregnancy test and found out that she's pregnant. We're both fifteen. What should we do?

Help

Dear Help,

I'm very sorry that you have to deal with this situation. You and your girlfriend have important decisions to make, and you're going to need all the support you can get.

The first thing you need is adult help. I don't know what kind of relationship either of you has with your parents, but I suggest you talk to the parent you think will be the most understanding. It won't be an easy conversation, but you can't ignore a pregnancy; this is too much for the two of you to deal with alone.

If you can't count on any of your parents or if there's not another caring adult you can talk to, call 1-800-230-PLAN, the national hotline for Planned Parenthood. By calling, you'll be transferred to the Planned Parenthood clinic closest to you. You and your girlfriend can make an appointment by phone to go to a clinic and get help sorting out your options. If you're not comfortable contacting Planned Parenthood, make an appointment with a doctor who can help you decide what to do.

I hope everything works out for you and your girlfriend, and I wish you both well.

In friendship,
Terra

Changing Bodies, Changing Lives: A Book for Teens on Sex and Relationships by Ruth Bell (New York: Times Books, 1998). This updated classic offers everything you want to know about sex, physical and emotional health, and personal relationships. With important questions and comprehensive answers, this book helps you make wise choices.

Like It Is: A Teen Sex Guide by E. James Lieberman and Karen Lieberman Troccoli (Jefferson, NC: McFarland and Company Inc., 1998). This frank sex guide covers the questions most teens have about sex, including birth-control options, infection and disease, and the emotional aspects of sexual relationships.

The Underground Guide to Teenage Sexuality: An Essential Handbook for Today's Teens and Parents by Michael J. Basso (Minneapolis: Fairview Press, 1997). Written in clear language (with lots of illustrations to make things even clearer), this conversational book offers helpful information about sex and sexuality.

Talk City's The InSite
www.talkcity.com/theinsite/me/some_body/me_sex.html
This section of Talk City's The InSite is all about sex, including the basics on reproduction, birth-control options, and sexually transmitted diseases, as well as information about sexual orientation. "Been There" stories tell what it's like to deal with STDs, sexual-orientation issues, and more.

Teen Wire
www.teenwire.com/
Teen Wire is Planned Parenthood's Web site for teens. Here you'll find information about dating, love, sex, sexual orientation, abstinence, birth control, puberty, and much more. An "Ask the Experts" section features real letters from teens. There's also an online teen zine called "Hothouse."

SEX AND EMOTIONAL RISKS

While the physical risks of sex (pregnancy and STDs) are easy to pinpoint, the emotional risks aren't. Why? Because people respond to situations differently. Something that may be exciting to one person may be frightening to another, and what may be emotionally devastating for you may be "no big deal" for someone else. You simply can't predict how you're going to feel. *Before* you find yourself in a romantic situation with things careening out of control, think through all the possible consequences *carefully*.

If you become sexually active before you're ready, you may feel over-whelmed and confused by the feelings that go along with this type of intimacy. This is especially true if you can't talk freely to your sexual partner about what's going on between you, how you feel about each other, what you're doing, and what the relationship means to you.

Sexual activities, *especially* sexual intercourse, leave people emotionally vulnerable. During sex, people tend to be less guarded with their feelings, which allows them to be very close to each other. Ideally, that closeness extends into the rest of the relationship. Until you've experienced this kind of closeness with another person, you can't really understand it, except to know that it can be very wonderful—provided you and your partner totally trust and respect each other. When you *don't* trust each other or don't know each other well enough to feel deeply respected, being intimate can leave you feeling hurt, betrayed, and alone.

If you and your boyfriend/girlfriend aren't sexually active but are consider-ing it, have a conversation about it before you find yourself in the "heat of the moment." For many teens (and adults, too), it's almost easier to have sex than to talk about having it. Unfortunately, many people get physical before they're emotionally ready. For this reason and many others, it's also smart to talk with an adult you trust about the choice you're facing.

Before you decide what to do about sex, you also need to talk to another person—yourself. *You* are the person who has to live with the consequences of your decisions, so be clear about what's right (and wrong) for you. Ask yourself these questions:

- Knowing there are huge physical and emotional risks involved, why am I thinking of having sex?

- How do I think sex will change my relationship? Do I think it will make us love each other more? Why? Do I think it will make the relationship last longer? Why? Do I think we'll have more respect for each other? Are my expectations realistic? Why or why not?
- Is having sex consistent with my values (the "right" or "wrong" choices for me)?
- Is my choice to have sex consistent with my parents' values? If they find out, how will it affect my relationship with them?
- If I decide to have sex, what kind of contraception am I planning to use to guard against pregnancy and STDs?

You may want to write your answers to these questions in your private journal. It will help you think about things more clearly. Consider all of your choices, and remember to listen to your inner voice, which will always tell you what's right for you (see pages 6–10 for how to do this).

What if you're in a sexual relationship now and you're not certain what to do? First, make sure you're fully aware of all the physical risks involved and take any necessary precautions. Talk to your partner: are you both comfortable with the relationship as it is? If you're not involved with anybody at the moment but you have had sex in the past, don't assume that you have to jump into another sexual relationship. You can abstain from sex anytime. It's *always* your choice.

If you've never been sexually active, don't give in to pressure to do more than you're ready for. See "Where to Turn" on pages 100 and 105 for more information about sex and its physical and emotional consequences.

How do you know when you're ready for sex?

Hey Terra,

My boyfriend and I think that we're ready for sex, but how can we tell for sure?

Ready

Dear Ready,

Before doing anything, ask and answer the following questions (you may want to write the answers down so you can think about them later, too):

- How do you think sex will change this relationship? How might it change the way you feel about your boyfriend? How might it change how he feels about you?
- Do you completely trust your boyfriend and his feelings for you? Does he completely trust you and your feelings for him?
- Are you willing to risk pregnancy and/or getting a sexually transmitted disease?
- How will you feel about yourself if you become sexually active?
- If you have sex, how will you feel if the relationship ends (which it probably will eventually, because most teen relationships do)?
- What expectations will your boyfriend have after you "do it"? (Will he expect to have sex whenever you're alone? Will he be jealous if you talk to other guys?) The best way to get the answers to these questions is to ask him directly.

As you can see, there are lots of questions to consider, and you're the only one who can answer them. So, take your time to think things over. A healthy decision is one that's 100 percent right for you and the person you're thinking of having sex with. Be sure to ask yourself what your values really are. Listen to your inner voice!

In friendship,
Terra

My girlfriend and I ended up having sex, but I didn't want to

Hey Terra,

The other night, I didn't want to have sex with my girlfriend, but she kept, you know, touching me and I got an erection. Even though I told her no, she wouldn't stop. So we ended up having sex, but I didn't want to and now I feel really weird, embarrassed, and kind of upset about what happened.

Unwilling Will

Dear Unwilling Will,

When your girlfriend didn't take no for an answer, she wasn't treating you with respect. Just because your body responded to stimulation and gave you the ability to have sex doesn't mean you wanted to do it. Part of the reason you're upset and confused is that you feel betrayed by your girlfriend and by your own body.

What should you do about it now? Tell your girlfriend how upset and embarrassed you feel about what happened. You deserve an apology. Make sure your girlfriend knows that the only way you'll continue this relationship (assuming you want to) is with the understanding that the two of you will respect each other's wishes at all times.

If you need to talk about your feelings with someone other than your girlfriend, I suggest you talk to a school counselor or another trusted adult and explain what happened. Thanks for writing.

In friendship,
Terra

I don't want to have sex, but I don't want to lose him!

Hey Terra,

My boyfriend and I have been going out for two years. I love him a lot, but we have a problem. He's been asking to have sex with me, and it's getting to be a regular argument between us. I keep telling him that I don't feel ready for that kind of relationship, but he keeps trying to convince me that it would be great because we'd get so much closer. I'd like us to get closer, but I don't want to do something I'm not ready for.

He says there are lots of girls who'd love to have sex with him. How does he know that? Is he flirting with other people? Are other girls offering? I think if he really cared about me, he'd want to be with me even without the sex—don't you agree? I don't want to have sex with him, but I don't want to lose him either.

Stuck

Dear Stuck,

Having sex with someone because you're afraid to lose him would mean having sex for the wrong reason. If you do it anyway, you may lose respect for yourself. Also, having sex with your boyfriend doesn't guarantee that he'll stay with you.

After two years together, it's natural for a guy to want to have sex with his girlfriend (depending on how old you both are). Your boyfriend is experiencing intense sexual feelings and may not know how to channel that excess energy in nonsexual ways. But it's *his* responsibility to deal with that without pressuring you. You don't have to justify your decision to anyone, and you don't have to do something you're not ready to do.

Your boyfriend's pressure isn't a good sign. A healthy relationship is based on mutual respect, and you deserve more respect than he's giving you. I agree with you, if he really cares, he should want to be with you whether you have sex with him or not. Tell him that you don't appreciate the pressure and that if you're going to continue the relationship, he needs to slow down. If he doesn't, you may have to break up with him and move on. Be strong and be true to yourself. Good luck!

In friendship,
Terra

The First Time: What Parents and Teenage Girls Should Know About "Losing Your Virginity" by Karen Bouris (Berkeley, CA: Conari Press, 1994). In this book, women of all ages and races share their stories of their first sexual experience. These stories offer information, advice, and a unique look into the emotional aspects of having sex.

Teen Love: On Relationships (Chicken Soup for the Teenage Soul Series) by Kimberly Kirberger (Deerfield Beach, FL: Health Communications Inc., 1999). This book for teens offers advice for sorting out the feelings that come with romantic relationships. It includes original letters from teens, wise advice, and insights about falling in love and handling your desires and feelings.

UNHEALTHY RELATIONSHIPS

Healthy relationships are based on honesty, trust, respect, and open communication. They're also *balanced*. That means both people treat and regard each other as *equals*.

When one person feels more important, loved, and in charge, the relationship isn't equal. It's unbalanced and unhealthy. If you're in this type of relationship, it's time to talk, make changes, or move on.

Unhealthy relationships are more likely to occur when:

1. There's a large age difference between partners. The older person, who has more life experience, tends to dominate.

2. One person is more "in love" than the other. The person who's more in love may be afraid of losing the relationship. The other person sometimes uses this fear to manipulate and control the relationship.

3. One person is abusive. This can include verbal, emotional, physical, and/or sexual abuse. Abusive relationships are the most unhealthy and dangerous kinds.

What exactly *is* abuse? It's mistreatment of any type and can range from insulting "jokes" to violence. In a relationship, the abuser (the one who's mistreating the other) feels superior to the abused.

The abuser may exert control in many different ways. For example, an abuser could say mean and hurtful things (verbal abuse). Or gain control by constantly ignoring or purposely hurting the other person's feelings (emotional abuse). Or use violence or threats of harm to get his/her way (physical abuse). Or force someone to perform a sexual act (sexual abuse). In each case, the abuser treats the other person with a tremendous lack of respect.

Why are some people abusive? And why do some people tolerate abuse? These are difficult and complex questions. Teens who have been abused by a parent or caregiver may grow up mistakenly believing that this behavior is part of a "loving" relationship. For teens in this situation, abuse might feel "normal" or inevitable (as if there's no other way), and they may not know how to express love in an appropriate manner. In fact, these teens may even become abusers themselves.

Some teens who are currently in relationships in which they're mistreated haven't been abused before. Still, they may be attracted to or involved with people who treat them poorly. Once they're caught in the pattern of abuse, they may find it very difficult to get out of the painful relationship. Or they may become abusive themselves because they don't understand what it means to treat someone with respect.

Abusive relationships are very confusing because the mistreatment may occur infrequently or at random. These relationships often go through cycles; for example, one minute the abuser lashes out and the next minute acts apologetic and sweet. Because the abuser may also be very loving at times, it can be difficult for this person's partner to leave the relationship. He/she may hold out hope that the abuser will never act out again and will continue to be loving.

Low self-esteem also keeps abused partners from leaving unhealthy relationships. On some level, the abused person believes he/she deserves to be mistreated or "punished." The person doesn't *want* to be abused (nobody wants that) but doesn't feel worthy of fair and loving treatment. The person may think he/she provoked the abuse and may have mixed-up feelings about love and violence. These feelings and beliefs are deeply rooted and need to be resolved through counseling.

Abusers rarely stop and become healthier without professional help. More often, the abuser gets more violent and disrespectful as the relationship goes on. This makes it even harder for the abused person to leave. He/she may feel threatened, worthless, and totally alone.

To find out if you're in an abusive relationship, answer the following questions:

1. Are you unhappy with your boyfriend/girlfriend because you feel he/she is controlling you?
2. Do you do things you don't want to do because you feel intimidated by your boyfriend/girlfriend?
3. Do you feel terrible about yourself because of things this person says to you?
4. Does your boyfriend/girlfriend push you around or threaten to hurt you?
5. Does he/she hit you?

6. Does your boyfriend/girlfriend force you to engage in sexual intercourse or other kinds of intimate behavior?
7. Do you do any of the above to your boyfriend/girlfriend or anyone else?

If you answered yes to any of questions 1–6, you may already be in an abusive relationship. You can take steps to work things out or leave the relationship. If you answered yes to number 7, you may be an abuser yourself, and you need to stop this behavior. It's very hard to do this alone, so you may want to talk to an adult about getting help.

It's never okay for anyone to hurt you or for you to hurt anyone else. But whether you're an abuser or are being abused, you can learn to make better choices in the future. The pattern *can* be broken. If you think you're in an abusive relationship or you know someone else who is, you need to:

• talk to a school counselor or other trusted adult,
• call your local YMCA or YWCA to ask about workshops on abuse awareness and prevention,
• look under Women's Services in the Yellow Pages and call an organization that offers domestic violence-prevention services, or
• contact one of the organizations in the "Where to Turn" resources below

It will take hard work and persistence to resolve these issues. But it can be done!

National Domestic Violence Hotline
1-800-799-SAFE (1-800-799-7233)
This English/Spanish hotline is open twenty-four hours a day, seven days a week. The people who answer the phone are trained in crisis intervention, and they can refer you to a teen violence-prevention program in your area. You can also use this hotline if you have a friend or family member in an abusive relationship and you want tips on how to talk to this person and offer help.

RAINN (Rape, Abuse, and Incest National Network)
1-800-656-HOPE (1-800-656-4673)
www.rainn.org
RAINN, started by musician Tori Amos, is a nationwide clearinghouse for organizations dealing with issues of sexual and physical abuse. A call to RAINN will
automatically connect you to the rape crisis/domestic violence-prevention
center nearest you, so you can get help and counseling.

My boyfriend is totally mean to me

Hey Terra,

My boyfriend, who I love more than anything, is totally mean to me. He calls me names, and
he shoves me around. He says stuff like, "You're a fat bitch" and "You're too stupid to understand." He says he loves me, but if you love someone how can you say stuff like that?

Hurting

Dear Hurting,

People who consistently put down, embarrass, or lash out at others have serious problems.
They try to control people by being insensitive or by using verbal or physical abuse. You can't
change your boyfriend's behavior, but you *can* take care of yourself.

Ask yourself why you're in this relationship. Although you may love your boyfriend, you
most likely don't love the part of him that's mean to you. If you don't feel good about who
you are, you may believe that you don't deserve to be treated well. Or maybe you think you
deserve cruel treatment because you feel guilty or ashamed about something you've done.
Talk to a school counselor or another adult who can work with you to get to the root of your
feelings and help you understand that you deserve respect.

I also recommend that you end this relationship, so you can put energy into understanding yourself better, figuring out what you need, and learning to stick up for yourself. You can
tell your boyfriend, "I have to break up with you because I feel bad a lot of the time when I'm

with you, especially when you call me names. I feel scared and hurt when you shove me around. I need to leave, so I can feel good about who I am." No matter how hard he might try to convince you to stay, you need to do what's best for you. And that means staying away from him. I suggest that you bring a friend or two with you when you break up. That way, you won't have to worry as much about your boyfriend getting violent.

Make sure you get help from other people. Talk to friends who know about your situation, and reach out to an adult who cares about you. I hope this helps!

In friendship,
Terra

I'm afraid to ask my girlfriend what's going on with her

Hey Terra,

My girlfriend used to be a sweetheart, but lately her whole personality has changed. I wish I knew what was going on with her, but I'm afraid to ask. She doesn't like it when I ask her personal questions. The other day, I just asked her what she wanted to do this weekend and she got all mad and started yelling at me, saying that she'd let me know when she decided and that I should quit bugging her! So I guess I'll just keep quiet and wait until the girl I fell in love with comes back again, because right now she's scary to be around.

Chilling

Dear Chilling,

Being controlling (by saying things like, "I'll let you know when I decide. Quit bugging me!") is a type of verbal abuse. Even though your girlfriend may not be physically violent, she's using a form of emotional control. You should never have to feel afraid of someone you're in a romantic relationship with.

The solution isn't to keep quiet and wait until things change. Healthy relationships are balanced and have open communication. Talk to your girlfriend about her behavior. You might say, "I'm not happy with the way things have been going. I feel like you yell at me all the time, and I'm not having fun in this relationship anymore. I know something's bothering you, and I'd really like to talk about it." If you need some support before you tell her how you feel, find a counselor or another caring adult who can help. You could invite your girlfriend to be part of this conversation, too. Her behavior could be a sign of a deeper problem, and it may be helpful for her to talk to an adult. I wish you both well.

In friendship,
Terra

My boyfriend questions my every move

Hey Terra,

When my boyfriend and I got together a year ago, everything was positively heaven. Then this new guy "Doug" came to our school. He's a real player, and he also drinks. My boyfriend and Doug became friends, and my boyfriend started acting just like him. He showed up at my house drunk, and when I told him that he couldn't come in, he started yelling at me. He later apologized, but then he did something worse—he slept with this other girl! I was extremely hurt, but he apologized, and I forgave him.

Things got better, but then he started getting really jealous and asking me questions about everything I did when I wasn't with him. Also, he tells me who I can hang with and where I can go. It's like I can't even breathe without telling him about it. He says that if I ever talk to another guy, he'll beat the you-know-what out of me and the guy. My friends can't stand him, and they tell me that I should break up with him, but they don't understand how much I love him. What should I do?

Southern Girl

Dear Southern Girl,

You know in your heart that this isn't a healthy relationship. Do you really want a boyfriend who calls all the shots and is jealous, possessive, cheating, drunk, controlling, and out of control? I suggest that you take a hard look at his behaviors—they're a form of abuse. Your boyfriend needs professional help to deal with his problems.

Ordinarily, I'd encourage you to tell your boyfriend how you feel when he behaves abusively. But in this case, I don't think he'd listen. Your words might just make him angry, which could put you in danger.

I agree with your friends—they have your best interests at heart. End this relationship as soon as possible. Meet your boyfriend in a public place when you tell him that it's over, and bring a friend or two with you (so you're safer). Make a clean break and don't look back. You deserve to be treated with much more respect than this guy can give you! I wish you the best.

In friendship,
Terra

He loves me, but he hits me

Hey Terra,

My boyfriend hits me a lot, even though he really loves me. I know I should break up with him (even though I love him) and I have, lots of times, but he always gets me to go back with him by telling me how sorry he is and that he'll never do it again. But he always does. Last week, he pushed me really hard against the wall, and I bruised two ribs. I know it was my fault because I said something about his car, and he got really mad. When my mom asked me what happened, I lied to her and told her I fell down the steps. How can I get my boyfriend to stop being so rough?

Tired of Hurting

Dear Tired of Hurting,

This guy hits you and has bruised your ribs—this is abuse! You can't get your boyfriend to stop being rough with you; he has to get professional help for that to happen. If you stay with him, your life and health are in danger. I want you to know that it's definitely not *your* fault that he behaves this way. He has a problem.

I know this is hard to hear, but you need to get out of this relationship before you get even more seriously hurt. You're 100 percent right when you say that you need to break up with him. This time, make it *for good*.

Tell your mom or another adult you trust the truth—today! Then talk with this adult about how you can break up with your boyfriend safely. Take precautions by bringing an adult or some friends with you when you tell him good-bye. Take care.

In friendship,
Terra

SAYING GOOD-BYE

Sometimes you suddenly fall in love and then, just as suddenly, you fall out of love. Emotions are unpredictable and can change without warning. Even though your feelings may take you by surprise, you have choices about how you deal with them. Your inner voice (see pages 6–10) will tell you the right thing to do.

Most people think relationships end as a result of changing feelings. Although this is sometimes true, people more often break up because they aren't willing to talk about their emotions. Instead of openly communicating, many people sweep their feelings under the rug. Pretty soon, all the little unspoken resentments, hurts, and insecurities create such a lump in the rug that no one can walk over it without tripping.

So what do you do now? You can't ignore that growing lump forever! It's a good idea to lift up the rug, take a look at all those feelings you've been hiding, and talk about what's bothering you. Many people do just the opposite, though, because they figure it's easier to toss out the rug and get a new one. As a result, the relationship ends, and one person is left feeling shocked and hurt, while the other probably feels guilty. And *neither* person learns much about how to have a healthy relationship.

Lots of issues can cause lumps (problems) in relationships. These include disrespect, dishonesty, a lack of trust, and a lack of communication. To avoid these relationship pitfalls, *talk* to your boyfriend/girlfriend whenever a conflict arises. This way, you get things out in the open. Communication can lead to solutions.

But what if you *have* talked about the problems and have even tried to solve them? Maybe you seem to keep arguing about the same old things or you feel "stuck." Or maybe your wants and needs have changed, and the relationship isn't headed in a direction you're both comfortable with. When this happens, it may be time to move on, even if you still care about each other.

Breaking up is never easy, because no one wants to be the "bad guy." Some people stay in relationships longer than they really want to, just to avoid having that awful "good-bye" conversation. I once had a friend who wanted to break up with her boyfriend. When she started to tell him how she felt, he got so upset that he began to cry. His tears broke her heart, and she let herself be talked out of her decision. This couple ended up getting married but, unfortunately, there wasn't a happy ending. The marriage lasted for only a few years, and by then, they had a baby daughter. They really didn't belong together in the first place, and my friend knew it. They should have broken up, but instead they got married. The eventual breakup (a divorce) was much more painful than the original split would have been.

The truth is, all breakups are painful, and hurt feelings are bound to occur. If one person doesn't want the relationship to end, he/she is going to feel upset. Rejection hurts, but the feelings don't last forever. One way to make a breakup a little easier is to be honest and sensitive. If you're the one ending the relationship, don't:

- lie about why you're doing it
- let someone else break the news
- stop talking to your boyfriend/girlfriend, instead of breaking up
- do something to trigger a breakup, like cheating or being abusive
- exaggerate the problems in the relationship to the point where you've convinced yourself that your boyfriend/girlfriend is so awful that you can't figure out why the two of you ever got together in the first place

None of these methods is a healthy or fair way to end a relationship. Just because you've had a change of heart doesn't mean it's okay to be unkind. And lying won't actually "spare" anyone's feelings (it usually just makes the situation worse). Your boyfriend/girlfriend deserves to hear the truth. After all, if someone was breaking up with *you*, you'd want honesty. If the person were to simply stop talking to you or to lie, you might always wonder what went wrong. This can make it much harder to get over a broken heart.

When you're sure that it's time to say good-bye, keep these tips in mind:

1. Remember that it takes two to make and break a relationship. Feelings aren't completely one-sided in a relationship. If you're unhappy, for whatever reason, the other person is probably feeling the same way.

2. Be aware of your feelings. Before you talk to your boyfriend/girlfriend, identify your feelings. You may feel frustrated, jealous, or trapped. Whatever feelings you have, they're yours and they're valid; you don't need to make excuses or apologize for them.

3. Be honest. Once you understand your feelings, communicate them with your boyfriend/girlfriend. This conversation isn't about blaming the other person for what he/she did or didn't do. Depending on the particular issue you're dealing with, you might say something like:

"I'm feeling trapped in this relationship. I feel like we spend too much time together, and there are other things I want to be doing, on my own and with other people. I don't want to be your boyfriend/girlfriend anymore."

"I'm feeling ignored, like my opinions and ideas aren't all that important to you. I want to be treated like an equal, and to be with someone who cares about me but isn't embarrassed to show it. You're not the right person for me right now."

"I'm sorry, but I'm no longer attracted to you in the same way that I used to be. You have many great qualities, and I had a lot of good times in this relationship. But now I want to see other people."

When you speak honestly about your feelings and treat people with sensitivity and respect, you might discover that difficult conversations aren't as hard as you had imagined. And when you talk, you might even discover that you *both* sensed that the relationship wasn't working.

I don't like her as much as I used to

Hey Terra,

I think I might be losing interest in my girlfriend. I'm not sure what it is, but I just don't like her as much as I used to. Part of me wants to break up with her, but she's a really nice person and I would hate to hurt her. What should I do?

Stumped

Dear Stumped,

You're pulling away from your girlfriend, but you're not sure why. Looking at the history of your feelings might reveal some answers.

Remember the good times that you and your girlfriend had together and how you felt when you were with her then. You once liked her a lot, or she wouldn't be your girlfriend. When did your feelings start changing? Can you pinpoint a particular moment when something happened between you? It could have been a fight or something your girlfriend said or did. Maybe at the time you pushed your emotions aside and pretended everything was fine, but deep down the feelings were still there. Unresolved feelings can put distance between people.

Talk to your girlfriend honestly and tell her about your changing feelings. Give her a chance to express her emotions as well. The two of you may still break up, but if you treat your girlfriend with honesty and respect and let her know how you're feeling, you both can learn something important about healthy relationships. Good luck!

In friendship,
Terra

What's going on with my boyfriend?

Hey Terra,

My boyfriend has been acting weird lately. We used to spend more time together than we do now. And when we're together, he spends a lot of time talking about his ex and how sexy and cool she is. I've been hurt by guys a lot in the past, and my boyfriend knows that. And even though he swears that he'd never hurt me, I wonder why he's talking about her so much. I'm really worried.

What's Up?

Dear What's Up,

If your boyfriend knows that you've been hurt by guys a lot, he may be afraid to tell you how he's really feeling. His lack of attention and his talk about his ex could be his way of slowly ending your relationship.

I suggest that you ask him to be honest. The longer he hides things from you, the harder it will be to reveal the truth. Take the lead and ask your boyfriend to talk openly about the future of your relationship. If he admits that he has romantic feelings for his ex, you may feel hurt and rejected, but at least you'll know where you stand. If you get the support you need after a breakup, the hurt will heal much faster. Talk to your friends or a trusted adult about your feelings, instead of bottling them up. Take care.

In friendship,
Terra

I'm not happy with my girlfriend, but I don't want to be alone

Hey Terra,

I've been with my girlfriend for a couple of months, which is twice as long as any other relationship I've ever had. At first, we both liked each other the same (maybe I liked her a little more), but now it's the complete opposite. She tells me she loves me all the time. I don't dislike her, but I'm sure not in love with her. I'm not the kind of person who would say it if he didn't mean it, so I feel really uncomfortable with her telling me that all the time. The other thing is that there's really no one else that I like, so I'm not sure it's so smart to break up with her because then I won't have a girlfriend. What should I do?

She Loves Me

Dear She Loves Me,

It's hard to let go of the person who loves you, but at the same time, it's unfair to hold on to someone you don't truly care for. You may be leading your girlfriend to believe that you feel the same way about her, even though you haven't actually said the words, "I love you." If you're honest with your girlfriend and tell her you're not in love with her, you might either pave the way for a new level of communication between you or cause a breakup. If the relationship ends, you'll be alone for a while, but at least you'll know you were truthful and had the courage to stop pretending about a relationship that didn't mean that much to you. I hope this helps!

In friendship,
Terra

My boyfriend thinks I'd be perfect if I'd only change a few things

Hey Terra,

My fantastic boyfriend and I are getting serious (we're both nineteen), and we've been talking about marriage. The problem is that we're so different that I'm wondering if it can work. I'm a pretty quiet person and he's really an extrovert, and he wishes I'd be one, too. Also, he says that I need to lose about ten pounds and be more willing to try new things, like go with him to watch kick boxing, which I don't really care about. If I can change the things he doesn't like about me, it will be perfect between us. I guess I'm willing to do that, but I'm a very honest person, and there's a part of me that believes that changing my personality would be a form of lying. It brings me down to think about it because, if he really loved me the way he says, he wouldn't want me to change. I could just be me, and that would be fine with him. What do you think?

Just Me

Dear Just Me,

Your boyfriend may be a great guy, but he's probably not great for you. You shouldn't have to change yourself to please someone else. In a healthy relationship, both people accept each other's differences. If your boyfriend can't appreciate the thoughtful, honest, straightforward young woman you are, he's not "Mr. Right" for you. I think it would be a mistake to marry a guy who wants to change you.

Be true to yourself! Talk to your boyfriend and tell him how you're feeling. You may discover that the solution is to go your separate ways. If this happens, it's for the best. Someday you'll meet a guy who will love you exactly as you are. In fact, *who you are* will be what he loves most about you. I wish you well.

In friendship,
Terra

My girlfriend told people we broke up, but we didn't!

Hey Terra,

I love my girlfriend very much, and I thought she felt the same way about me, but I just heard that she told some people that we broke up. It's not true! I asked her if she said that we broke up, and she told me she was just kidding when she said it. She's really beautiful and very popular, and I wonder why she's with me, but she says that she loves me and I want to believe her. I don't know what's going on here, and I'm having trouble trusting her. So could you help me, please?

Needing Help

Dear Needing Help,

I don't blame you for wondering what's going on here. Your girlfriend spreads the word that you two are "history," and then she says she was only kidding. (The people she talked to obviously didn't think she was kidding!) Telling others about your supposed breakup may have been her way of sending a message to you.

If she isn't interested in being your girlfriend anymore, encourage her to be honest about it. You deserve the truth. You sound like a very loving person, but you can't hold a relationship together by yourself. Healthy relationships are a two-way street. Both people have to work together to make their relationship healthy and balanced. I hope this helps!

In friendship,
Terra

Can I break up with my boyfriend without hurting him?

Hey Terra,

My boyfriend is a very sweet guy, but I'm just not in love with him anymore. I want to break up, but I don't want to hurt him. Is there an easy way to do it without hurting him?

Gentle Soul

Dear Gentle Soul,

I'm glad you understand that your feelings have changed and it's time to move on, and I think it's very caring of you to be concerned about your boyfriend's feelings. Unfortunately, there's not an easy way to tell him that you don't love him anymore, but here's some advice that might make it a little less painful for both of you:

1. **Talk to your boyfriend face-to-face.** Communicate your feelings honestly.
2. **Stick with "I feel . . ." statements.** These are easier to hear than "You never . . ." or "You always. . . ."
3. **Act with sensitivity.** Your boyfriend is probably going to feel upset, so be kind.
4. **Make a clean break.** Don't let yourself be talked out of your decision.
5. **Say thank you.** Tell your boyfriend what this relationship has meant to you.

After you say what you need to say, leave. That way, he can be with his feelings in private. Good luck!

In friendship,
Terra

GETTING OVER A BROKEN HEART

Having someone break up with you can be a very painful experience. Even if you aren't madly in love with the person, it's natural to feel rejected when you hear the words, "I want to break up with you." You might have suspected that the relationship wasn't working, or you might have thought everything was going fine. Either way, when someone says good-bye, it can come as a shock.

What should you do if someone breaks up with you? First, ask your boyfriend/girlfriend to be honest about what's going on. You might ask, "Why do you want to break up?" This will make your bf/gf stop and think about the reasons. Understand, though, that the person breaking up with you is probably feeling as uncomfortable as you are and may want to avoid a long conversation. In fact, he/she may want to get away from you and be alone, and you might feel that way, too. If you're upset by the news, spend some time by yourself. Later, when both of you are calmer, talk about what happened, if the other person is willing.

I vividly remember being "dumped" by my boyfriend when I was sixteen. There was no "I don't think we should see each other anymore" announcement. Instead, he stopped talking to me and completely ignored me. I couldn't figure out why his feelings toward me had changed (I still don't know). What I *do* know is that I was terribly confused and hurt by the experience. He wasn't a bad person—he just didn't want to deal with my reaction. I'm sure that if he'd had the maturity to be honest and direct, this would have softened the blow. I still would have been upset, but at least I wouldn't have wasted so much time and emotional energy wondering what happened.

If you've been dumped, you know how much it hurts. (You may be hurting from those feelings right now, in fact.) What can you do to get over the pain? Before you look for a quick fix, it's important to realize that you've suffered a loss. With the loss of any close relationship, you need time to grieve. A period of grieving is natural and healthy, and it gives you the chance to mourn the relationship you've lost.

After you've felt your sadness for a while, start thinking about letting go and moving on. No one can tell you how much time you should spend grieving, because each person handles these feelings differently. Just be aware that if your sadness over a breakup takes control of your life and the loss becomes the only thing on your mind, you may be "stuck" in your grief (in which case you may need to talk to a school counselor or another adult who can help).

That old saying "Time heals all wounds" is true. The painful feelings gradually subside, but they may continue to affect your future relationships. Instead of waiting for the hurt to fade, deal with it now by following these tips:

1. Talk to your ex in person. Communicate your feelings honestly so you can release them. Don't try to cause a guilt trip or win him/her back. If either of you gets angry or out of control, stop the discussion immediately and get away from each other. If your ex acts very friendly toward you or even comes on to you, don't assume this means he/she wants to get back together. You could end up hurt again.

2. Write a letter. Communicate your feelings in the letter. (You won't mail it, so you can be totally honest.) How did you feel in the relationship? How do you feel now? Describe what you did to contribute to the breakup.

3. Write a letter from your ex to you. After you've finished the first letter (above), pretend that you are your ex and write a reply letter. If you allow yourself to really get into it, you might discover things you never realized before.

4. Seal both letters in an envelope marked, "Don't open till . . ." (Fill in a date that's one year from the date you write the letters.) Stick the envelope way in the back of your closet or in some drawer you hardly ever open. Someday, you'll reread the letters and realize how far you've come from where you are now.

If you don't feel better after these writing exercises, perhaps you haven't expressed everything you need to. If so, write another letter to your ex and another letter back to yourself. The goal is to get some closure, or feel "complete."

After you've tried some (or all) of these suggestions, ask yourself how you're feeling. Check in with your body to see if you need food, water, sleep, fresh air, exercise, or a shower. It's just as important to take care of your physical health as it is to take care of your emotional health.

The last step in getting over a broken heart is to determine what you've learned from the experience. Relationships (even ones that end sadly) are great opportunities for self-discovery. Talk to someone you trust about how you feel.

My boyfriend says he doesn't know why he dumped me

Hey Terra,

I just got off the phone with my boyfriend a few hours ago, and he dumped me! I can't believe it. Everyone said we had the best relationship of anyone in our school. I thought so, too! When I asked him why he was breaking up with me he said, "I don't know." Is that possible?

What Happened??

Dear What Happened,

When a guy backs out of a good relationship and says he doesn't know why, there are a few possible explanations:

- He's hiding something.
- He's afraid of intimacy (so the closer you get, the more he wants to pull away).
- His track record makes him distrustful of romantic relationships, so he decides to initiate the breakup before you dump him.
- He's fallen in love with someone else.
- He truly doesn't know why!

   I don't know which, if any, of these, is accurate in your case, but it seems to me that if the relationship was as great as you thought it was, someone isn't being honest. Sounds like you need to have a conversation with your ex. If you make it safe for him to talk (without interruptions or a guilt trip), he may be able to tell the truth about his decision to break up with you. Let him know how you feel about the situation. You may not get back together, but you'll know that you handled yourself with honesty, maturity, and self-respect. Good luck!

In friendship,
Terra

I'm having a hard time getting over my girlfriend

Hey Terra,

My girlfriend broke up with me seventeen days ago at a party. I knew that this other guy in our class liked her, but whenever I asked her if she liked him back, she said no. I guess she was lying. Now I feel like nothing she ever said to me was true. So even when I asked her what I had done to cause her to break up with me, she said, "Nothing. You are very sweet." If I'm so sweet, how come she's with him now? Maybe if it doesn't work out with them, she'll come back to me. If she doesn't, I don't know what I'll do. I'm having a really hard time here, and I was wondering if you could please help.

Lost and Loving

Dear Lost and Loving,

A broken heart can heal, but it takes time. I'm sure it's not easy to see your ex and her new boyfriend every day at school. To make matters worse, you're wondering if your girlfriend was lying to you throughout the relationship. The only way to find out is to ask. Talk to your girlfriend about her reasons for breaking up with you. Once you know, you can begin to let go.

After a breakup, it's normal to feel hurt and to long for things to go back to the way they were. Get support from friends or an adult you trust. Soon, you'll be ready to begin the next chapter of your life. Call some friends that you might have been too busy to spend time with when you and your girlfriend were together. Make plans to do things you enjoy. A great way to get over a heartbreak is to start some new activities and relationships in your life. Thanks for writing.

In friendship,
Terra

I miss my ex, and I want her back!

Hey Terra,

My ex and I broke up over something really dumb. She's going out with someone else right now, and they're very serious with each other, but he's not right for her at all. Besides, I still love her and when she looks at me, I just know that she still loves me, too. I even dream about us being together again. How can I get her to break up with her boyfriend and get back with me?

Take Me Back

Dear Take Me Back,

I understand that you still care for your ex, but it's hard to say for sure if she feels the same way. She's dating someone else now, which means it's time for you to let go. If the two of you broke up for a "dumb" reason, it may be worth telling her that you're open to the idea of getting back together someday. Don't push the idea, though. Once you've had your say, move on with your life.

Get involved in a hobby you've always wanted to learn about or a sport you want to get better at. Stretching your mind and body in new directions can take some of the strain off of your broken heart. These activities will also offer opportunities to meet new people. As time goes by, you may meet another girl you'd like to ask out, or you may come to realize that your breakup with your ex was a positive thing. Good luck!

In friendship,
Terra

My girlfriend dumped me

Hey Terra,

My ex broke up with me because she met this older guy who drives a '97 red Ferrari. Obviously, he has lots of money, plus he's a superjock at a private school. How can I compete with all that?

Left Out

Dear Left Out,

Your letter explains your assessment of why your girlfriend broke up with you: the other guy is older, has more money, and drives a cool car. Wait a minute! If this girl cares so much about those things, she was the wrong one for you.

 Some people care more about what a person "has" than who a person "is." If finding someone who shares your values is important to you (and I hope it is), look for this type of girlfriend. Someday, you'll find her! Best of luck!

In friendship,
Terra

I'm not over him yet

Hey Terra,

My ex-boyfriend wasn't very nice to me; in fact, he was abusive. That's why when we broke up, I wasn't too sad about it. But the thing is, I haven't had a boyfriend since then (almost a year), and I miss being close to a guy. So whenever I'm lonely (which is often), I think of the nice memories I have of me and my ex, and I even think about calling him up. But I know that's dangerous because of the past abuse. Anyway, I'd like to get over the anger and hurt.

So, is there any way I can just be friendly with him? I mean, he's a human being, and we ought to be able to be friends, right?

Feelings Haven't Died

Dear Feelings Haven't Died,

There's no "rule" that says you need to be friends with or even friendly to someone who has hurt you. Sometimes it's better to leave those people behind and get on with your life. You're still angry and hurt, which is natural; express these feelings in your journal or by talking to people who care about you. When you're lonely, find a friend or a family member to spend time with. Don't let feelings of loneliness lead you back into a hurtful relationship with someone who abused you.

It sounds like breaking up with your ex was the best thing you could have done. Congratulations! To fix your aching heart, go out and do things you love to do—sports, hanging out with friends, after-school activities, or whatever makes you feel excited and happy. Leave the past behind and move forward with your life. Thanks for writing.

In friendship,
Terra

How can I get him to love me again?

Hey Terra,

This guy I really liked broke up with me. My feelings for him are as strong as ever, so how can I get him to love me again?

Heart Broke

Dear Heart Broke,

I'm sorry the guy you like doesn't feel the same way about you anymore. Unfortunately, there are no such things as love potions to get people to fall back in love (and besides, such potions wouldn't make someone really love you for *you*). Instead of thinking about ways to win him back, spend your energy developing new interests. Maybe there's something you've always been interested in learning more about—yoga, video production, ceramics, whatever. Now would be a great time to find an after-school class through a community center, a YMCA or YWCA, or a local university. Start looking forward to the rest of your life!

As hard as it is right now, believe me, letting go will get easier in time. To speed up the healing process, express your feelings. A broken heart lasts longer when you don't release the hurt, anger, loneliness, or betrayal you feel. You don't have to share any of your feelings with your ex (unless you want to), but you *do* have to get them out. I wish you well.

In friendship,
Terra

CHAPTER 5

friends

Friends, Peers, and Enemies

he family members or caregivers you grow up with are really your first "friends." If these relationships were healthy, you learned early on about the joys of connecting with another person. Connecting with others is a basic human need, and that's why as soon as you started school, you began developing friendships outside of your family.

By the time you're a teen, the role your friends play in your life takes on a deeper meaning, both socially and emotionally. Life is more fun when you share it with friends, and your problems are a little bit easier to handle when you've got someone to talk to. But what about friendships you're not so sure of? What happens when friends grow apart or if one of them turns out to be untrustworthy?

What about your peers—the people you see nearly every day but who aren't necessarily your friends? What role do they play in your life? Or the people who seem like enemies and enjoy making you miserable? What do you do about *them*?

Dealing with friends, peers, and enemies—while very challenging—offers you great learning opportunities. When you know how to make the most of these challenges, you can become a more confident person and a better friend.

REAL FRIENDS VS. THE OTHER KIND

We all need friends. People are social creatures, and we like being around others.

Good friendships allow you to feel more secure, and by giving you the freedom to be yourself, they help you enjoy life more. Friendships also help you become more aware of what you want and need in a romantic relationship (which may, someday, lead you to a life partner). While romantic relationships obviously aren't the same as friendships, the healthy ones have *friendship at their foundation*. So, if you learn the basics of being a good friend, you have a better chance of developing healthy relationships with people you're interested in romantically.

You may call many people "friends," but some of them are definitely better friends than others. You can tell the difference between real friends and the other kind, because *real* friends:

- **respect** each other's values
- **talk openly** about what's on their minds
- **keep agreements** they make
- **support** each other
- **share expectations** about what friendship means

Most of all, a real friend is *someone you like*. Liking someone is the number one ingredient in a solid friendship. People are complex, and many different things attract us to others and make us want to get close. Maybe you've said or thought, "My friend sometimes acts very weird, but I like her anyway. I don't know why, I just do." Why you like a person can't always be explained (to someone else or even to yourself), but it doesn't *need* to be. Affection happens between people for all kinds of reasons, such as:

• **Instant likes.** When you instantly like someone, you might say it's because the two of you have good "personality chemistry." You might also see something in the other person that's similar to a quality you have. Most of us don't realize that our friends' positive qualities are often things we like about *ourselves*. Friends who share your strengths help you learn more about making the most of your best traits.

• **Instant dislikes.** If you immediately dislike someone, perhaps that person has a quality you recognize and dislike in yourself. If you look closely, you might realize that you're sometimes a little bit like that person, which gives you something in common. In fact, if you overcome your negative feelings for each other, you might even become friends, and this isn't a bad way for a friendship to start. By sharing your "weaknesses" and talking about them honestly, you can work together to turn them into strengths.

Real friends don't need to be totally alike or to agree about everything. But real friends *do* need to respect each other enough to talk about their decisions and give each other honest advice.

Do you have friends from various ethnic backgrounds who've had life experiences different from your own? If so, this gives you an amazing opportunity to grow. Maybe you've thought or said something like, "My friend and I come from totally different families, and sometimes the way we do stuff is the exact opposite, but none of that matters because we really respect each other." Such friendships can broaden your understanding of other people, deepen your compassion for all human beings, and help you appreciate what makes each person unique.

But when friends have different values and opposite ideas about right and wrong, it's more difficult to remain close. What can you do if your friendship is headed in this direction? Or what if you're starting to feel as if the qualities that once drew you to a certain friend don't appeal to you anymore? It's time for open communication! Talk so you can each share your point of view and figure out the next step.

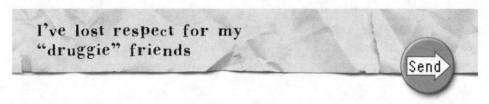

I've lost respect for my "druggie" friends

Send

Hey Terra,

Drugs are destroying my life, and I'm not even doing them—my friends are! It's not like my friends are forcing me to do drugs (they're not), but I have an uncle who's a drug addict so I have a real problem when I see other people doing drugs.

I think that my friends are being really stupid, and I've lost a ton of respect for them. But I still care about these people, and I don't want to lose their friendship. I just don't like being around them when they're stoned. So even though I don't respect the choice they're making, I don't feel like I should be the one telling them not to do this stuff. What should I do?

Anonymous

Dear Anonymous,

It's good that your friends aren't pressuring you to do drugs. Even though you don't like or respect their decision to use drugs, you have to accept that it's their choice. You can't force them to stop.

You've got a difficult decision to make, but you're intelligent and strong enough to make it. Set limits with your friends, for your own sake, and let them know how you feel about what they're doing. Tell them about your uncle to help them understand where you're coming from. Explain that you still care about them but that you've lost respect for them—and tell them why. Then say that you don't want to be around them when they're doing drugs. If you make them choose between spending time with you and doing drugs, the ball is in their court.

Maybe they'll change their behavior, but if they don't, you'll need to decide your next move (which may be finding new friends). I support your wish to have friends whose values you share and whose choices you can respect. I hope this helps!

In friendship,
Terra

I used to like this girl, but now I don't want her as a friend

Hey Terra,

This girl came to my school last year. She was new and I thought she was nice, so we became friends. Now it just seems like everything she does bugs me, and since she still doesn't have any other friends but me, I feel sort of trapped. The reason that she doesn't have any other friends is because she talks a lot and is always trying to impress everyone with stuff that she did at her old school. I don't want to be mean or anything, but I don't like her. She calls me all the time, and I just don't want to be friends with her anymore!

She's Driving Me Crazy!

Dear She's Driving Me Crazy,

You sound like a nice person, and I admire you for not wanting to hurt this girl's feelings. I also appreciate that you want less closeness with her because you are, as you say, feeling trapped. Even if you don't want this girl to be your friend anymore, she deserves respect—and that means clearly communicating how you're feeling.

You might say, "I know you don't have many other friends here yet, but it's starting to feel like we're always together and it's too much for me. I need time to do things with other people, and I wish you had other people to spend time with, too. Maybe if you tried to get to know other people besides me, you'd make some new friends." If you tell her the truth in a way that's meant to help and not hurt, you're giving her the opportunity to grow and change.

You're always free to end a relationship, and doing it honestly, with respect and sensitivity, is a mature way to resolve the issue. One more thing: you could talk to a teacher about the dilemma and maybe he/she could design a class project to get the girl involved with some new people. Good luck!

In friendship,
Terra

My two best friends are worst enemies

Hey Terra,

My two best friends don't like each other very much, which is weird because they were best friends long before I became friends with either of them. Anyway, I'd like for the three of us to be together, but that's impossible because they absolutely refuse to talk to each other. They don't mind talking *about* each other, though, and that's the part I hate the most. They both tell me all this bad stuff about each other. It would be so much nicer if they got along—then we could all do stuff together. Instead, I have to keep track of whose turn it is to be with me. Got any ideas about how I can get them to make up?

Sigh

Dear Sigh,

I'm sorry you're in the middle of all these negative feelings. Your friends are being disrespectful to each other and to you! But there's no law that says all of your friends need to get along with each other, even though it would be much nicer for you (and them) if they did.

Unfortunately, there's not much you can do to make peace between them, except to explain how it makes you feel for them to be enemies. You might say, "I wish you guys could be friends again, but if you don't want to be, then fine. I just want to tell you that I'm not going to listen to you criticizing each other anymore. I've heard enough of that. If you can't stop, I'll have to find other friends to spend time with." As long as they respect your request not to use you as a dumping ground for their hostilities, you can continue spending time with each of them individually. If they keep on "trashing" each other in your presence, stick to your promise to start spending time with more peaceful people. I wish you well.

In friendship,
Terra

My friend is having sex with her boyfriend!

Hey Terra,

My best friend and I used to be really close, and we'd tell each other everything. But about two weeks ago, she told me something I wish she had kept secret. She's having sex with her boyfriend! I'm a virgin, and I think premarital sex is wrong. Now that I know what she's doing, I've lost respect for her and I feel like I can't be her friend anymore. She still thinks we're best friends. What should I do?

Troubled

Dear Troubled,

It's important for friends to respect each other's values and choices. This is especially impor-tant for issues you hold close to your heart. Because you believe it's wrong for people to have sex outside of marriage, I understand why you've lost respect for your friend. But are you really ready to give up the friendship?

You're entitled to your feelings and it's your choice whether to remain friends with her. But if you haven't already done so, communicate your feelings to your friend. Otherwise, she's going to wonder what's going on, and it wouldn't be honest to pretend that nothing has changed when so much has for you. And it wouldn't be fair to create distance between you, without explaining why you've done so. Talk openly with your friend and listen to her point of view. Thanks for writing.

In friendship,
Terra

Communicating

One of the best parts of having a solid friendship is knowing that you've got someone to turn to when you really need to talk. Ideally, you and your friend should feel comfortable discussing just about anything with each other. Open communication is a basic element of all healthy relationships, but what hap-pens when it isn't there? It becomes more difficult to resolve problems.

When a friendship is going well, it's as if there's clear air between you. But if something bad happens, it's like an invisible glob pollutes that clear space. Maybe neither of you can see it, but you both feel its presence. When some-thing seems uncomfortable or "not right," you may be tempted to ignore it. Some-times it feels easier to end a friendship or let it fade away, rather than face conflicts directly. But it's a real test of your friendship (on the part of both people involved) to do what it takes to "clear the air." For information about working out problems, take a look at Chapter 9, "Conflict Resolution Tool Kit," on pages 229–237.

Resolving conflicts can be hard work, but good friendships are worth the effort. And if you put energy into working things out, you're more likely to have healthy friendships that last for years.

My friend won't talk to me about our fight!

Send

Hey Terra,

Sometimes my friend says stuff that hurts my feelings. At her surprise party last weekend, her mom had invited some friends of hers from camp. She was hugging them and screaming about how happy she was to see them (they live pretty far away). When I tried to give her a hug, she sort of pushed me away and said real loud, "I get to see *you* all the time." That made me feel like I wasn't very important to her and that it wouldn't have mattered if I wasn't even at the party.

At school on Monday, I told her how her remark made me feel, and she got all angry and said that I was trying to mess up our friendship. I said that I was sorry and that's *not* what I was trying to do, but she didn't want to talk about it and rushed off. She hasn't talked to me in two days. What do I do now?

Feeling Hurt

Dear Feeling Hurt,

I admire you for trying to work things out with your friend. However, it takes two people to "mess up" a relationship and two people to fix it. Clearly, you're willing to try, but your friend isn't yet.

Perhaps she needs some more encouragement. You could say something like this, "Our friendship is really important to me, and I don't want to lose it. Could we talk about what happened?" If she agrees, set up a time to talk. Be sure to pick a time that's good for both of you (right before a test won't work). Also, choose a place that's private, so you're both free to share your feelings without worrying about anyone overhearing or interrupting.

If she still won't talk, give her space. If she values the friendship, she'll probably reach out to you after she cools off. On the other hand, if open and honest communication isn't something she can handle in a relationship, then she isn't the kind of friend you can count on.

If things don't work out between you and you feel lonely and want to meet other people, find new ways to spend your time. Make a list of things you enjoy doing, and then think about the activities that are available in your school and community. There are lots of new people you can meet who may offer exactly what you want and need in a friendship. I hope this helps!

In friendship,
Terra

My friend has no idea what's going on with me

Hey Terra,

My friend is constantly making assumptions about what's going on between me and my girl-friend. He has this weird idea that she's manipulative and is using me. He saw us once when we were in the middle of an argument. She was saying some stuff about how she would go back with her old boyfriend if I didn't get her two dozen roses and a really awesome gift for her birthday. She was just kidding around, but my friend thought she was serious.

Me and my girlfriend have a really good relationship, and there's no way that she's using me. If my friend knew anything about my relationship, he wouldn't even think that.

Misunderstood

Dear Misunderstood,

Has communication between you and your friend gone bad? If so, why? Has your relationship changed since you've gotten a girlfriend? He may feel left out and even a little jealous of the time you spend with her. Also, because he cares about you, he doesn't want to see you get hurt, and you can't blame him for that. Maybe you're not talking to your friend about your girl-friend, which is why he's making assumptions about what things are really like between you.

I suggest that you tell him why you care for your girlfriend and explain that you really do respect each other. Invite your friend to spend time with the two of you, and then he can see for himself that the relationship is healthy. Keep the lines of communication open between you and your friend, so your friendship stays strong. Just because you have a girlfriend now doesn't mean you don't need other friends anymore. I wish you well.

In friendship,
Terra

I told my friend that I'm a lesbian

Hey Terra,

I'm fifteen, and I've known that I'm a lesbian for about a year. I came out to some online friends, and they were all cool with it, so I decided I'd tell my best friend. I don't have romantic feelings for her—I just wanted her to know the truth. She freaked and called me awful names, and she said that she didn't want to have anything to do with me anymore. I feel really hurt about this because we've been best friends since we were eight. I don't understand why she's acting like this. We've had talks about homosexuality before, and she always said she didn't have a problem with it. Obviously, she does have a problem with it. Is there anything I can do to have her be my friend again?

Lavender Girl

Dear Lavender Girl,

You were brave to come out to your friend. It was a risk, and I'm very sorry you were hurt. Your earlier discussions about homosexuality gave you the impression that your friend didn't have a problem with it. But sometimes people have one opinion when they talk about things in general and a different opinion when the topic affects them personally.

Your friend's reaction is prejudiced. Her opinions are blinding her to the fact that you're still the good friend she's always cared about. I suggest that you give her time to think. It's likely that she may realize she's overreacting. I hope, for your sake as well as hers, that she discovers your friendship is what's really important. Give her another chance to figure that out.

Some people will accept you as a lesbian, and some people won't. Acceptance is something everyone deals with, gay or straight. The people who love and accept you are your *real* friends. Always remember that.

Many schools now have gay-straight student alliances, or organizations that bring gay and straight people together to fight ignorance and build bridges between them. These groups often have newsletters or Web sites to offer support. Ask your school counselor for more information about organizations to contact. Maybe you can even start a gay-straight student alliance in your own school. Good luck!

In friendship,
Terra

Resource Guide to Coming Out

www.hrc.org/ncop/guide.html

This site is published by the Human Rights Commission. Elizabeth Birch, HRC's executive director, says, "No one should be denied the opportunity to thrive and flourish as a full human being because his or her sexual orientation is different from that of the majority." The resource guide presents information about homosexuality, advice on coming out (to yourself and others), and a list of additional resources including organizations, books, and online links.

Youth Resource

www.youthresource.com/queeryouth/

Youth Resource is a project of Advocates for Youth, an international organization dedicated to meet the reproductive and sexual-health needs of young people. The Youth Resource Web site is filled with personal coming-out stories and wonderful art. It also includes information about making your school safe from prejudice and violence.

MAKING AND KEEPING AGREEMENTS

Agreements are promises or understandings between people. You and your friends probably have lots of agreements; some of these are spoken, like a verbal promise to always be available to talk. But many agreements are unspoken ones, like sticking up for each other or not telling each other's secrets. Whether spoken or unspoken, agreements should be respected and honored. This allows you to build trust and to strengthen your relationship.

Suppose you and a friend agree to meet somewhere. You're there on time, and so is your friend. You've both kept your agreement, and you feel good that you can count on each other. But what if your friend doesn't show up? That's a *broken* agreement. You might feel confused, hurt, and maybe even a little worried that something bad happened to your friend. Assuming nothing bad happened, what should you say when you see your friend next? If your friend rarely breaks agreements, a simple apology and an explanation is really all you need.

But some people break their word almost all the time. In fact, some people can hardly ever be depended on. Even if your friend means well and offers a reasonable excuse each time an agreement is broken, you're getting the message that you just can't count on this person. When you continue trusting someone who's untrustworthy, you're in for regular disappointments. Someone who consistently breaks agreements isn't a real friend.

When agreements are broken, it's your responsibility as a friend to tell the person how you feel. Find out what happened and work together to make sure things are handled differently next time. When friends discuss problems as they occur—instead of letting hurts, resentments, and a lack of trust build up like a pile of junk under a bed—the friendship becomes stronger and both friends grow in positive ways.

She didn't get me a birthday present

Hey Terra,

When a best friend promises to do something, she ought to do it, right? And if she breaks that promise, maybe she isn't such a great friend after all, right? This happened to me when my friend promised she'd get me a gift for my birthday and didn't. It's not that I care all that much about the gift, but I feel really hurt that she broke her promise. I'm kind of disappointed since she told me that the thing she was going to get me was so cool.

Giftless

Dear Giftless,

Tell your best friend how you feel. She might not even be aware that you're disappointed. And unless you talk to her, you won't find out why she didn't give you a gift. Perhaps it's a money issue, or maybe she's having second thoughts about how cool the present is and doesn't want to give you something you'll be disappointed in. Don't assume that the reason she didn't give you the gift is because she doesn't care about you anymore.

If you put distance between you instead of talking about what happened, you may be throwing away a great friendship. That would be a much greater loss than not getting a birthday gift. I wish you well, and Happy Birthday!

In friendship,
Terra

He promised not to tell

Hey Terra,

My friend has made my life hell for the past two weeks. First, he told the girl I have a crush on that I like her after he swore he wouldn't. Then he spread the news all over school. Now this girl who used to be so nice and friendly to me is totally avoiding me, and all of her friends are saying she thinks I'm some kind of "player." This situation is really bad, and it's all my friend's fault. What's even worse is that he says I never told him not to tell anyone, which is an absolute lie! I'm so mad that I can't even talk to him!

Steamed

Dear Steamed,

Because you've already told your friend how you feel and why, I'd recommend taking some time to cool off. If he doesn't apologize, it may be better to end this friendship.

Some people seem to enjoy stirring up trouble, and they never take responsibility for the problems they cause. Does this sound like your friend? If so, it's likely that he'll continue to tell your secrets and hurt you again. On the other hand, maybe he thought he'd be helping by telling the girl you like about your feelings. You'll never know until he's ready to admit the truth. Good luck!

In friendship,
Terra

We made a pact not to mess around with each other's boyfriends

Hey Terra,

I can't believe the mess I'm in, but my two best friends wouldn't be friends anymore if one of them knew what the other one did. I wish I didn't know, but I do. You see, I just found out this afternoon that my friend "A" slept with my friend "T's" boyfriend. "A" told me this herself, and then she begged me to keep my mouth shut and I agreed. I know this isn't fair to "T," but what am I supposed to do? When the three of us became best friends in sixth grade, we made this pact that we'd *never* mess around with each other's boyfriends, not even after one of us broke up with him—and certainly not when one of us was still going out with him! What should I do about this mess?

In a Mess

Dear In a Mess,

What a totally unfair position for "A" to put you in! Tell her that you aren't going to lie for her anymore. She has broken a major agreement with "T," and "T's" boyfriend has betrayed her, too. I don't blame you for not wanting to be a part of this secret.

I suggest that you tell "A" you're removing yourself from the middle of this situation because you don't want to take sides. Recommend that she admit the truth, because "T" is going to hear about it from someone else anyway. Secrets like this don't stay secret for long. If she refuses to tell the truth, let her know that *you* will. "T" deserves to know what really happened.

Betraying a friend is a sure way to bust up any friendship, a lesson that "A" needs to learn. Meanwhile, "T" will need some support, and you can give it to her. Remember to take care of yourself while you're dealing with all of this. Thanks for writing.

In friendship,
Terra

Support

Healthy friendships are a two-way street, in which both friends feel that their concerns and opinions are of equal importance. *Support* plays a big role here, too. In real friendships, both friends get their needs met and are able to grow in healthy ways.

For example, if your friend has a class presentation to give and wants to try it out on you first, you'll probably take the time to listen and offer some feedback. And because your friendship is a two-way street, your friend would do the same for you. If your schedules are tight and you can't always be there for each other, you both can offer support in other ways. Real friends do their best to be available to each other—but are understanding if something prevents this from happening.

Sometimes the kind of support needed by friends is of a much more serious nature. In potentially life-or-death situations, just "being there" isn't enough. Have you or a friend ever dealt with the kind of intense emotions that come from facing major life changes such as death, divorce, drug abuse, eating disorders, or depression?

You notice that your friend has been really down for the past few weeks, ever since his girlfriend broke up with him. You're worried because your friend seems out of it and isn't acting like himself. He doesn't return your calls or do anything with you after school anymore. When you ask him if something's bothering him, he responds, "Just life. It's all so pointless, I'm actually thinking of killing myself, just to make a change." He says it like a joke and then quickly remarks, "Just kidding. Don't get all worried about me." You want to help, but he doesn't seem to want to talk about what's on his mind. Should you just leave him alone until he works things out for himself?

In this situation, your friend is putting distance between you because he doesn't want to communicate. Maybe he's embarrassed to talk about how sad, rejected, or lonely he's feeling right now. Or maybe he doesn't know how to put his feelings into words. As a result, he's pushing you away, even though you're making an effort to show you care. Part of you may feel angry that your friend doesn't seem to want you around. But sometimes being a friend means offering support to someone who's hurting too much to ask for help.

It's natural for a person to feel down or depressed after a breakup. But, in this case, your friend's feelings are more serious. Anytime a friend talks about suicide, *take it seriously* and get some adult help. Reach out to a parent, a teacher, a school counselor, your principal, a religious leader, or anyone else you trust to handle the situation. If you can't find a trusted adult to talk with face-to-face, call a crisis hotline to talk to a trained counselor.

The Power to Prevent Suicide: A Guide for Teens Helping Teens by Richard E. Nelson, Ph.D., and Judith C. Galas (Minneapolis: Free Spirit Publishing Inc., 1994). This practical guide explains the causes of suicide, how to recognize the warning signs, and how to reach out to save a life.

American Suicide Survival Line
1-800-SUICIDE (1-800-784-2433)
This crisis hotline, staffed by trained counselors, is available twenty-four hours a day, seven days a week.

Boys Town National Hotline
1-800-448-3000
You can call this crisis hotline anytime, twenty-four hours a day. You'll talk to a professional counselor who will listen and give you advice on any issue (suicide, depression, and other problems). Online, go to: *www.ffbh.boystown.org/Hotline/crisis_hotline.htm.*

Support takes all forms, and the give-and-take isn't always exactly equal in a friendship (but it doesn't have to be). Friends might play different roles; for example, one person might usually give advice, while the other person seems to have all the problems. The relationship can still be a healthy, two-way street, as long as *both* friends know they can get support when they need it. What happens if the friend who usually gives the advice has a problem and needs help—can this person get advice from the friend who usually plays the role of "listener"? If not, the relationship is more like a one-way street. In a real friendship, the flow goes in *both* directions.

She says she'll call back, but she never does!

Hey Terra,

My friend has a boyfriend, and I don't. Maybe that's why I'm a better friend to her than she is to me. All I know is that whenever she's upset with her boyfriend or wants to tell me all the cool stuff they do together, she calls me to talk, and I listen. But whenever I need to talk to *her*, she gets off the phone really quick or she says she'll call me right back, but she never does! I've told her lots of times that I don't like it, and she always says she's sorry but then does it again.

Left Hanging

Dear Left Hanging,

I'm sorry that your friend is being insensitive. Some people have difficulty balancing a romantic relationship with their friendships. It's too bad when this happens, because people who do this tend to feel very lonely when their romance ends and they discover that their friends are gone, too.

It looks to me like this girl doesn't want to put the time or energy into a real friendship with you. Instead, she expects that you'll always be there when she needs you, even if she offers nothing in return. This is a set-up for you to keep getting hurt.

I suggest that you reach out to others in friendship. Are there some single girls or guys in your classes or that you see during after-school activities? Look around and decide who looks like they have high "friend potential." Most people are friendly, and they respond to a smile. Why not try it out and see what happens? You deserve to have friends who can give as well as take. I hope this helps!

In friendship,
Terra

I want to stand up for my friend

Hey Terra,

I'm white, and my best friend is Latino. We always stand up for each other. Yesterday, when he wasn't around, I overheard these jocks talking about him and calling him disgusting names that had to do with his race. They also talked about "surprising" him some night and letting him know that he wasn't welcome in our school.

As I listened to them, I felt scared for my friend and really angry, too. I started thinking about getting a knife and "surprising" them some night. I'm not a violent person, which is why I was shocked by how I felt. I probably would never mess with these guys, because they're much bigger than I am and might kill me, but how can I help my friend?

Peaceful

Dear Peaceful,

You're loyal, and your friend is lucky to have you to count on—especially since some people at your school aren't open-minded or respectful. It's natural to feel angry toward the guys who threatened your friend. I'm glad, though, that you didn't act out in violence. This shows maturity and an awareness of how important it is to be a peacemaker.

My suggestion is that you *immediately* talk to the principal or a school counselor about the threats you overheard. It's really important for a school official to be aware of what's going on inside the minds of these guys. That way, the school can talk to them, and you wouldn't have to put yourself in danger. (Ask to remain anonymous, so these guys won't know it was you who overheard their threats.)

The truth about racial prejudice is that it stems from ignorance. I would encourage you to use this experience as motivation to start a dialogue in your school about racial diversity. Maybe you have a particular teacher who would help you get this type of discussion going. When people of all different ethnic backgrounds start talking about their feelings, they're sure to realize that, as human beings, we're all much more similar than we are different. I wish you well.

In friendship,
Terra

The Peace-It Together Community Center

phoenix.mcet.edu/peace/zine.html

The Peace-It Zine is a Web magazine containing poems, stories, and artwork submitted by teens who want to share their thoughts about and experiences of prejudice and violence. Through this site, you can get in touch with peer leaders and violence-prevention experts.

Youthlink

www.youthlink.org/

Youthlink, a project of the Foundation of America (a nonprofit charitable organization) encourages young people to stay true to their values, speak out against injustice, and stand up for their rights and beliefs.

People are spreading rumors about my friend

Hey Terra,

Some kids are spreading rumors about a good friend of mine who has been like my big sister since I moved here seven years ago. I know for a fact that the rumors aren't true, but even if they were, I wouldn't care because I was taught that most of the stuff people say about other people is none of their business. What can I do to help her?

Needs Help

Dear Needs Help,

It's great that you realize this girl has been a true friend and deserves your help. She's lucky to have a friend like you who's willing to stand up for her.

Rumors can be very hurtful, so it's important to try to stop them. Whenever you hear this rumor, defend your friend. You could say, "What you're saying isn't true, and you should stop spreading it around." Ask some of your other friends to help in the same way to stamp out this rumor for good.

Fortunately, rumors usually don't last very long (as people in the newspaper business know, yesterday's news just isn't as compelling). The more people work against the lies, the more quickly the rumor dies. I hope this helps!

In friendship,
Terra

Trust

Support goes hand in hand with trust. Real friends trust each other and feel confident that they're on the same "team." Knowing what's expected of you as a friend, and meeting those expectations, is what friendship is all about.

If you've ever seen an action movie, you've watched bad guys stalk someone. They do things like sneak around corners carrying concealed weapons and often aren't what they pretend to be. You can't trust these people or turn your back on them for a minute, because you never know what they're up to.

With friends, on the other hand, you can relax completely. You can turn your back, and even close your eyes if you want to, because a real friend will never hurt you. And a real friend knows you won't hurt him/her either. That's mutual trust, and you can count on it.

This isn't to say that mistakes don't happen in a friendship—they do. Sometimes people accidentally say or do things that hurt each other. When this happens, a good friend will admit the error and apologize. Good friends forgive each other and move on.

But what happens if a friend says or does something with the intention of hurting? That's called a *betrayal,* and it's a major break in trust. You might wonder, "Why would my friend do that to me? I'd never do something like that!" All of a sudden, the person you trusted isn't quite so trustworthy anymore, and you might feel very confused and insecure.

If a friend betrays you or if you betray a friend, it's important to talk about it. Even though the conversation might be uncomfortable, you and your friend have got to communicate. Here are some suggestions for talking things out:

• **Share your side of the story.** If your friend hurt you in some way, communicate this. Let him/her know how you feel and why. If you did something hurtful to your friend, explain why you did it.

• **Listen to your friend's side of the story.** If your friend betrayed you, find out why. After you've listened, ask yourself if you feel confident that you've heard the *real* reasons behind the actions. If you don't feel that the truth has been revealed, you may still have trouble trusting your friend, even if this person promises never to betray you again. If the betrayal was yours, on the other hand, listen to what your friend has to say to you. Don't get defensive.

• **Apologize and forgive.** This is an essential step for putting the betrayal behind you and continuing your friendship. Make a promise to each other that this will *never* happen again. Then keep your promise.

• **Decide whether you're still friends.** If a friend who has betrayed you can't guarantee that it will never happen again, the relationship may be damaged beyond repair. You no longer have an important ingredient for friendship: trust. If you betrayed someone, find out whether you're truly forgiven. Whatever you and your friend decide, be honest about what you're doing and why.

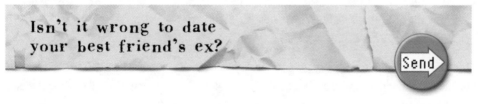

Isn't it wrong to date your best friend's ex?

Send

Hey Terra,

My best friend's boyfriend just broke up with her. They had gone out for eight months. The thing is that he and I have known each other since seventh grade (we're in ninth now), and

I've always had a crush on him. Now that he and my best friend aren't together anymore, he asked me out but I haven't said yes yet. It doesn't seem right. What do you think?

Waiting in the Wings

Dear Waiting in the Wings,

I agree that it doesn't seem right. Your inner voice is telling you that going out with this guy wouldn't be a good thing for you and your friend.

If the guy broke up with your friend, she's probably feeling awful. It's important for you to support her, and dating her ex wouldn't be supportive at all. In fact, going out with him could feel like a double betrayal to her. She might even start to believe that *you* caused the breakup. Be the best friend you can be while your friend is going through this tough time.

As for your feelings for this guy, keep them to yourself for now. Wait and see what happens after a few months. The guy you like is on the rebound right now, and he may feel like he needs to find someone to replace his old girlfriend. Give him some time to sort out his feelings. And keep listening to your inner voice!

In friendship,
Terra

I said something awful behind my friend's back

Hey Terra,

I made a mistake and said something that wasn't very nice about my best friend. She never would have found out, except that the guy I said it to told her. Now she's all mad and won't talk to me. Help!

Sorry

Dear Sorry,

Someone who's friends with you trusts that you'll always act like a friend. When you "trash" a friend, he/she can't help but feel betrayed, and that's what's going on here. You've learned the hard way how much it hurts when you break one of the ground rules of friendship.

What can you do about it now? Tell your friend face-to-face or write her a letter explaining why you did what you did. Maybe you were trying to impress the guy, or maybe you were getting back at your friend for something you think she did to you. Whatever the reason, apologize and assure her that it won't ever happen again.

I hope she'll forgive you. If not, you still learned a very important lesson about friendship. Good luck!

In friendship,
Terra

My best friend stole my girlfriend!

Hey Terra,

I went away on vacation with my family, and while I was gone, my best friend asked out my girlfriend. She said yes, even though we're only supposed to date each other. They went to the movies and a couple of other places. When I came back and found out about it, I was really shocked. At first, my girlfriend said it was "nothing," but then she broke up with me and started going out with my friend. That hurt a lot, but they seemed happy, so I didn't say anything. Then she dumped my friend, but I hear he still likes her. I still like her, too, and tonight she called and asked me out. Should I go back with her? What about my best friend— I don't want to hurt his feelings since he still likes her so much. What should I do?

Aaargh!

Dear Aaargh,

You're a very kindhearted young man. I must admit that I'm surprised you still consider this guy your best friend after he betrayed you like he did. You're concerned about hurting his feelings, but I doubt he was thinking about *your* feelings when he asked out your girlfriend. And speaking of your girlfriend, she hasn't proven to be very trustworthy, especially since you two had an agreement not to go out with other people.

If you're going to continue a relationship with both of these people, you need to have a serious talk with them and let them know how you feel about what happened. Tell them how hurt you are and ask them why they did what they did. You can either confront them both at the same time or talk to them separately. Do whatever you feel comfortable with.

One word of caution: being compassionate is a wonderful quality, but make sure that you don't let other people take advantage of you. You can stand up for what you know is right, communicate what you expect from a friend, and not lose one bit of your kindness and sensitivity. I wish you well.

In friendship,
Terra

What if your girlfriend's best friend comes on to you?

Hey Terra,

This may sound unbelievable, but my girlfriend's best friend came on to me. We were waiting in my car for my girlfriend to come out of school (we all carpool together), and this girl kissed me! I was really surprised, and I didn't kiss her back. Then my girlfriend got in the car, and her friend acted like nothing had happened. What's up with that? This is my girlfriend's so-called best friend!

RSVP

Dear RSVP,

I congratulate you for being a trustworthy boyfriend. Even though you were probably very surprised by what the girl did, you knew exactly the right thing to do (not to kiss back).

Of course, you don't want this happening again, so it would be best to talk to your girlfriend's best friend and tell her that you were really uncomfortable about what happened in the car and that you don't want it to occur again. You might say, "I love my girlfriend, and I would never do anything to hurt her. I'm surprised that you would think this is okay, since you're her best friend and if she found out, she'd be really upset with you. I just want you to know that if you do anything like this again, I'm going to tell her." If this doesn't stop her, I suggest that you tell your girlfriend what happened. She deserves a better friend than one who would betray her so easily. Good luck!

In friendship,
Terra

PEER GROUPS

Everyone has peers (people their own age who work or go to school with them) and feels pressure from them to some degree. Teens, however, usually feel it more strongly. Why is this? Most likely because, as a teen, you're trying to figure out what's important to you and what's worth standing up for. You're also trying hard to be accepted by others. This desire to fit in makes you more vulnerable to peer pressure. You may end up doing or saying something you don't want to because you're afraid of how others will react if you don't.

When most people hear the words "peer pressure," they imagine a noisy party where someone suddenly drapes an arm around a shy kid's shoulders and says, "Want a beer?" In this scenario, the kid could say, "No, thanks, I'm not thirsty right now" or "I don't drink" and walk away. There's another kind of peer pressure, though, and it's quieter and may be harder to resist. Suppose you wear your favorite old pair of shoes to school and overhear someone remark, "I wonder what century she got *those* in?" Maybe other people laugh, and you feel so embarrassed that you can barely think about anything at school that day. If you were to give in to that kind of pressure, you'd probably never wear the shoes to school again.

Still other kinds of peer pressure may not even be directed at you. Imagine, for example, that you're hanging out with a group of people and someone makes a racist, ethnic, sexist, or homophobic joke. Maybe you think it's offensive and not funny at all, but everyone else laughs. You might feel the impulse to laugh, too, even though the joke makes you uncomfortable or angry. If you *do* laugh, you've given into peer pressure. Even if you *don't* laugh but you don't speak out about the joke either, you've let peer pressure affect your actions.

What if this group happened to be your friends and not just a bunch of peers? Sometimes friends do things you're not comfortable with and problems arise. For example, what if they smoke and you don't want to? Or they wear clothes you can't afford and pressure you to dress the same way? What if they skip school, cheat, or shoplift? What if your friends treat other people poorly or make "rules" you disagree with? It's tough when friends do things that conflict with your own values. You find yourself in the awkward position of having to make a choice: follow the crowd or do your own thing.

No one wants to be without friends, but as you mature, you may realize that people who put negative pressure on you or expect you to compromise your values *aren't* real friends. They don't offer the affection, support, trust, and acceptance that real friends do. If you have to give up "friendships" that aren't real, you may feel lonely for a while, but you can find new people to get close to. In the long run, your path in life will be much smoother if you choose friends who share and respect your values.

My friend is pressuring me to be cooler

Hey Terra,

My best friend and I just started high school. There's this group of very popular girls from another middle school, and my friend thinks that if we try to be cooler, we can get in with them and the boys will like us better. She's into this idea way more than I am, and now that the popular girls are paying attention to her, she's pressuring me even more. Being cool is all she ever talks about, and I don't even care about it!

Probably Not Cool

Dear Probably Not Cool,

Everyone in the world has, at some point, wanted to be cooler or more popular. (Even the people who the rest of us think are already there!) Most middle-school students want to look and act just like their peers, and that's where the pressure comes in. Sometimes the attitude is that anyone who looks "different" is weird and to be avoided at all costs. Now that you're in high school, you're developing your individual identity. You might also start connecting with new peer groups that place a higher value on talents, interests, and activities, instead of on appearances.

You say that your friend is trying to make you cooler. If being cool means living your life by a certain formula, I agree that it's not worth the effort. If you and your friend do become accepted by the popular people, you'll start stressing out about "staying" cool enough for them. That's a waste of time and energy.

You know what? Being *really* cool means daring to be different and acting as an individual. The path your friend is on sounds more like conformity. If you feel good about who you are and are clear about your values, you'll be able to choose what's right for you, even if your best friend (or your entire peer group) chooses something different. Be true to yourself!

In friendship,
Terra

My friends are into things that I know are wrong

Hey Terra,

I feel stuck, and I hope you can help. My friends are into some stuff that I know is wrong (I'd rather not say what it is they're doing). They've already guaranteed that I'll be a social outcast if I refuse to do what they want me to do.

Witness

Dear Witness,

You haven't given me many details, but when it comes to peer pressure, the details don't really matter. Your inner voice is already telling you exactly what you need to do: stay away from things that you know are wrong. You have good values, and you're less likely to make a big mistake if you stick to them.

If these friends would dump you for sticking to your values, they're not real friends. You obviously don't feel comfortable going along with the things they do. But if you do what they say anyway, you're giving away the power you have over your own life. I understand that the idea of making new friends may seem scary. But it would be a whole lot worse to lose your self-respect than to lose these so-called friends.

Also, depending on how wrong the stuff they do is, going along with them may lead you into trouble. Do yourself a favor: before you make a decision, think hard about what's right for you. Picture how you'd feel if you were to do things their way. Then picture how you'd feel if you followed your inner voice. The only person you need to answer to is yourself. I wish you the best.

In friendship,
Terra

I'm not ready for all this boy stuff

Hey Terra,

I hear a lot about girls who have sex just because they're afraid they'll get dumped if they don't. I'm not ready for any of that stuff yet, but my friends are and they're always trying to set me up with friends of guys they're going with. I wish it could be the way it used to be with us, you know, before all the boy stuff started. I don't want to be a dork, but I don't want to get pregnant either!

Please Help

Dear Please Help,

I understand why you're wishing that your friends hadn't changed, but you're a smart girl who knows exactly what you are and aren't ready for. Real friends respect your values. All it should take is telling your friends to back off on the boy stuff until you're ready. You might say, "We've always been really good friends, and I know the reason you're setting me up with guys is so that we can all go out together. That's really sweet, but these guys aren't right for me. They want to have sex, and I'm not ready for that yet. So I'd really appreciate it if you'd stop pushing me. Okay?" If they're true friends, they'll get the message and stop bugging you about finding a boyfriend—and they'll still respect you and like you. On the other hand, if they continue to pressure you, I suggest that you find some single girls to hang out with. I'm sure there are plenty of them in your classes. Girls who aren't so obsessed with guys have a great time going out and doing things together. Have fun!

In friendship,
Terra

They want to keep picking on this girl, but I don't

Hey Terra,

This nerdy girl was bothering me and my friends. She did these really annoying things just to bug us, especially in science where she was always bringing in newspaper articles to impress the teacher. Anyway, me and my friends got tired of her talking to us like we were airheads, so we decided to get back at her. We started picking on her and putting mean signs on her locker and stuff. None of what we did was all that serious, but it probably wasn't very nice either. And even though she totally stopped talking to us, we kept it up. The thing is, I feel kind of guilty about it now, and I want to stop treating this girl so bad. But my friends say that if I do, they'll drop me.

Feeling Guilty

Dear Feeling Guilty,

Although it's very uncool to target someone because he/she is "nerdy," I admire that you now realize what you did was wrong. I also respect you for being ready to move on.

Begin by apologizing to the girl you've been picking on. Once you say you're sorry, and mean it, you won't feel so guilty anymore (and she may feel a little less hurt).

The next step is to talk to your friends. Tell them you've had enough of this juvenile stuff, and you aren't going to participate in the fight any longer. You might say, "I know that I was in on this thing at first, but it just doesn't feel right to me anymore. I'm not going to keep doing this, and I wish you wouldn't either. It's just not right to be so mean to somebody." If your friends want to continue, let them know it will have to be without you. That way, they get to choose.

One caution: if your friends aren't ready to grow up, they could turn their nastiness on you. (I hope this doesn't happen!) Be prepared and stay cool. You have good values, which can carry you through any situation. If things get really bad between you and your friends, I suggest that you talk to a school counselor or another adult who can give you ideas for resolving conflicts nonviolently. Good luck!

In friendship,
Terra

ENEMIES

The world would be a wonderful place if everyone got along, but unfortunately, that isn't the way life is and it probably never will be. The good news is that most people in your life are either close friends, friendly acquaintances, or people you don't have feelings for one way or another because you don't know them very well. However, some people may simply not like you, for whatever reason. Usually, they make their feelings known, and you may feel the same way toward them. If the feelings are very negative, you might even consider these people to be enemies.

How do people become enemies? Most often, they start out as friends, but then there's a fight, a major disagreement, or a betrayal. The conflict isn't resolved, and the two people start disliking, or even hating, each other. Sometimes people who were once the best of friends become worst enemies.

If you have a falling-out with a friend, you should try to put the conflict behind you. Unfortunately, you may not always succeed. It's not that you *can't* resolve the conflict (acknowledging a wrongdoing and saying you're sorry usually does the trick), but, in some cases, you may not be willing to do so. Maybe one or both of you isn't ready to let go of your feelings of hurt and anger. Holding on to the hurt and making the other person "wrong" somehow becomes more important than repairing the friendship.

When this happens, your friendship may just fade away, and you simply become former friends. Other times, the unresolved conflict grows and takes on a life of its own. The bitterness between you grows, and you form a new relationship: enemies. You may give each other the silent treatment, or you may say rude things to and about each other. It's terrible to waste energy hating each other. If you're in a situation like this, see Chapter 9, "Conflict Resolution Tool Kit," on pages 229–237. If all else fails, ask a school counselor for advice.

Not all enemies are former friends. Sometimes people who don't even *know* each other become enemies. These people might decide, after one look, that they dislike each other. What kind of thinking is behind a decision like this? Not clear thinking, that's for sure!

Too often these days, when teens take out their hatred on people they regard as enemies, schools turn into violent places, and innocent people are injured or killed. This is why it's so important to be aware of what's really going on in your school and in your community. Look around. Are there outcasts at your school—people who are left out, snubbed, picked on, teased, or even tormented? Have you witnessed racism, sexism, homophobia, or other forms of intolerance? Does your school have a bunch of cliques that exclude some students or make them feel terrible about themselves?

If you see "enemy" situations like this, speak out. Talk to your principal, teachers, school counselor, or any other adults who will listen. Get involved in your school's peer mediation program or find other ways to resolve conflicts peacefully. By joining together to make the peace, through community activism and student leadership, you can help teach your peers and the adults around you that life is too short for hating.

How can I get this guy to leave me alone?

Hey Terra,

There's this kid in my school, and we used to hang out together when we were younger. He's changed a lot, though. He used to be really nice, but now he always seems ready to pick a fight with me or something. He plays football, and I'm not into sports at all. Every time he sees me, he says stuff like, "Hey faggot! Where's your boyfriend?" I've never done anything to him, and even though I have a good friend who's gay, I'm straight. When my friend and I are together, the stuff this other guy says is even worse (I guess you can imagine).

Anyway, this guy is driving me nuts, but it's hard to avoid him because he's in two of my classes, and we take the same bus. Got any suggestions to get this guy to leave me alone?

What Can I Do?

Dear What Can I Do,

This kind of behavior is very maddening. It doesn't matter if you're gay or not, you deserve to be treated with respect, and so does your friend. I wish there was something you could say to this bully, something to get him to treat you with the respect you deserve. It's not likely, though, that anything you say will transform him into someone with maturity. (With any luck, time will teach him to be a more sensitive person.)

You shouldn't have to put up with his verbal abuse. Tell him, "I don't like the things you say to me. I want you to leave me alone." Go to your school counselor immediately and explain what's been going on. Then ask that something be done about it. If this guy is homophobic, others in your school might be, too. This would be an excellent opportunity to bring these prejudicial attitudes out in the open, so people can talk about their feelings and learn to be more accepting of differences.

I also suggest that you tell your parents about the situation, so they can talk to the other kid's parents. (Since you used to be good friends, your parents might know his parents. Even if they don't, a phone conversation is appropriate.) All of this may sound like "ratting" to you, but with so much violence occurring in high schools across the country, harassment needs to be taken very seriously. I sincerely hope your parents and your school will take action to support you. I wish you well.

In friendship,
Terra

Why did my friends turn against me?

Hey Terra,

I have a problem that I hope you can help me with. In my class (I'm in sixth grade), there's a group of girls that I used to be friends with. But one of them is having a party and hasn't invited me. When I asked her why, she said it was because the party is going to be "coupled up" and I was an "extra." Then this other girl said that the real reason is that none of the boys wanted to be coupled up with me. Now all these girls do is talk about the party and how cool it's going to be, and I feel really left out. What I don't understand is why they're being so mean. What can I do to get to go to the party?

Not Invited

Dear Not Invited,

A similar thing once happened to me, and I remember that it really hurt. But when I finally realized that the girls who snubbed me weren't really my friends, I stopped feeling bad. I know this can be confusing. Maybe you're wondering why these friends are treating you this way, or you're trying to figure out if you did something to make them turn against you. My guess is that you didn't do anything "wrong." Sometimes tight groups of friends find it "fun" to exclude others. They feel more important if they believe they're on the inside, while other people are on the outside. Of course, it never feels good to be excluded, but the inside/outside stuff is only as important as you make it.

So what can you do now? Well, unless these girls suddenly become more sensitive and compassionate, you probably won't receive an invitation to this party. How you feel about that is your choice. You can feel sorry for yourself, or you can use this as an opportunity to think about what makes a real friend. Look for an ally in your class—someone who isn't part of this clique of girls—and reach out to her. You and this other person already have something in common. If it feels like there's potential for a new friendship, I'd suggest that you plan something special to do, just the two of you, on the night of the party. This way, you'll realize that you have the power to create your own good time. Thanks for writing.

In friendship,
Terra

GROWING APART

In the same way that you can outgrow clothing, you can sometimes outgrow certain friends. People who were best friends in fifth grade may rarely talk to each other in seventh grade. People who didn't have much in common in sixth grade may become best friends in eighth. And people who were friends way back in elementary school may suddenly renew a friendship in high school.

Why do some of your friendships change like this? There's a simple explanation: it's because you probably change more during your preteen and teen years than at any other time in your life. And so many changes happening so quickly are bound to affect your friendships.

Try on a favorite shirt from last summer, and you may be disappointed that it's too tight, but you probably won't be shocked. You certainly won't "blame" the shirt for not fitting anymore, because you're used to this kind of growing and you've come to expect it. But there's another kind of growing that happens to you on an emotional level, and it's not always obvious to others or even to yourself. You may not realize you've changed, until you start reacting to old friends in totally new ways.

You're on an emotional ride toward adulthood, and as the years go by, you'll start seeing the world differently and experiencing all sorts of new feelings. These changes help you move forward in life. As you grow up, you'll start relating to your parents in new ways. You'll become more of an individual with your own values, opinions, and point of view.

As for friendship, you may spend years with the same people doing the same stuff after school and every weekend. Then one day, you may find that these activities no longer seem fun. Or maybe something your friend does, which used to seem cool, now irritates you. Or suddenly your best friend, who always called you a few times each day, isn't calling anymore. While this may be confusing, it's completely normal. The young adult you're becoming just has less in common with the kid you used to be.

What can you do about all these changes? Not a lot—except admit that you're changing. Talk about your feelings with your friends and listen to what they have to say. Do you still share some interests? If so, continue doing those activities together. If you both feel the friendship is over for now, acknowledge the good times you had and part on good terms.

Any friend who has ever meant something to you is a part of who you are today. If you cherish the memories of good friendships, you'll always remember these people fondly.

My best friend isn't interested in me anymore

Hey Terra,

Ever since my best friend "Sandy" and I started high school, I can't really say that she's my best friend anymore, though I've really tried to keep the relationship going. It's just that she's hanging out with other people who are way more mature than me. I think they're more mature than Sandy, but she says that's just my opinion. Anyway, she spends all her time with them, and she isn't interested in doing stuff with me and it hurts. I thought we'd be best friends forever and that our children would be best friends. What happened?

Nowhere

Dear Nowhere,

People change as they enter the world of high school. They find new friends and new activities. This isn't always a bad thing, though sometimes feelings get hurt. Stick with the friends you enjoy being with—the ones you can count on and who share your values and interests.

It sounds like you've already talked to Sandy about your feelings. Maybe you need to have one final conversation with her to find out whether she thinks your relationship is worth saving. If she isn't interested in remaining friends on any level, you'll know you've done everything you could do. You'll probably feel sad for a while, but if you keep busy with other people, the hurt won't last as long.

It's possible that your friendship with Sandy could be rekindled sometime in the future. You don't need to count on that, but you never know what's down the road. Maybe after time spent apart, you'll discover how much you miss each other. Or maybe you'll discover that you no longer have much in common. In the meantime, find new friendships that you can count on. I wish you the best.

In friendship,
Terra

My old best friend is acting like she doesn't like me anymore

Hey Terra,

My best friend has been like part of my family for eight years. Even our parents are good friends. Two years ago, we moved to another state for my dad's job. My friend and I wrote to each other a lot, and she came here for two weeks last summer. I also visited her during Christmas vacation. Now my family is moving back to my old town, though I'll be going to a new school. My friend will be at that school, too. But now, all of a sudden, she acts like she doesn't want me as her friend anymore. I don't know anybody else at the school, so what am I going to do?

New Kid

Dear New Kid,

Although you and your friend have continued communicating and seeing each other occasionally, that's not the same as going to the same school every day. Two years is a long time. You've changed a lot during that time and so has she. This is just a guess, but maybe your friend felt in competition with you and when you left, she didn't have to deal with that anymore. Now that you're coming back, she might be experiencing some of that old rivalry you never knew about. Or perhaps she's made new friends in your absence, and she somehow feels as if she can't be friends with both you and them at the same time.

Of course, you won't really know what's going on with her until you're settled in your new home and you have a chance to talk to her about her feelings. For now, give your friend the space she obviously wants. In a few weeks, invite her over to talk and listen to what she has to say.

As for you, there's lots to do to get ready for the move. While you're packing, imagine yourself in the new school, where you'll have opportunities to meet new people and make new friends. This is a chance for you to start fresh. Because you know how to be a true friend, uld be easier. Good luck in your new school!

ndship,

CHAPTER 6

Getting Along with Parents

In case you've never thought about it, being a parent* isn't an easy job. Maybe your parents have mentioned this once or twice, or maybe you've observed it on your own. Why is parenting so difficult? Partly because it doesn't come with a job description—parents often don't know what to do when their children (especially the first one) reaches each new phase of life. And sometimes parents make mistakes.

When you were younger and your parents made a mistake, you probably didn't notice. You (usually) accepted that they were in charge, and you probably never considered questioning their parenting skills. As a teen, though, you're probably scrutinizing everything they do. When they make an error, you might be quick to point it out to them. At the same time, they may be pointing out all of your "mistakes," such as poor grades or questionable friendships, for example. All of this finger-pointing adds stress to the relationship on both sides.

---

*In this chapter and throughout the book, I use the word *parent* or *parents* to indicate the adults you live with who take care of you. You might not have two parents or even one. You may live with stepparents, grandparents, foster parents, or relatives. No matter who's taking responsibility for guiding you through your first eighteen years of life, they *are*, in a sense, your parents.

Your relationship with your parents may be rocky at times, but you don't have to let it continue to go downhill. You can work toward building a healthy relationship by understanding each other better. This will help make your years at home more peaceful for your entire family.

Parents have to perform the tough balancing act of encouraging their kids to become independent while, at the same time, standing by ready to help when needed. This allows kids to grow up confident that they have a safety net in case they stumble or fall. Encouraging independence and being supportive are two ways that parents show love for their children.

The vast majority of parents love their kids and want the best for them. If you have trouble accepting that, perhaps it's because your own experience tells you it isn't true. Maybe you have a parent who left you, or is very ill, or spends a lot of time working, or has a drug or alcohol problem. All of these are reasons why this parent isn't really there for you. Maybe you have a parent who won't give you any breathing space or allow you to get emotionally close at all. Maybe physical abuse occurs in your family, and that creates a frightening mix of emotions—none of which are supportive or encouraging.

If you're living in such a situation, you need to get help, if you haven't already. Talk to a school counselor, religious advisor, or another trusted adult— and do it today. Family problems make growing up so much more difficult, and you deserve a chance to work through these issues with the help of someone who cares.

If your parents, for whatever reason, aren't giving you the emotional support you need, you don't have to grow up without it. You deserve to have at least one honest, helpful, supportive adult in your life. (If you can find more than one, that's great!) If you can't find these people in your family, look for them elsewhere. Reach out to people who are good listeners, are willing to tell you the truth, and want to make a positive difference in your life.

The kind of person you're looking for is called a *mentor*, someone who can help you work on problems and identify and reach your goals. Here are some places to find a mentor:

• **Within your own family:** Talk to older siblings and adult relatives.

• **At school:** Talk to your school counselor, advisor, favorite teacher, principal, or coach.

• **At your place of worship:** Talk to your religious leader, youth group leader, or other available adults.

• **Through friends:** Talk to a friend's parents, or ask your friends for mentor recommendations.

• **Through mentoring organizations:** Contact Big Brothers Big Sisters of America, Boys & Girls Clubs, or the YMCA or YWCA. Your local phone book should have listings for these organizations.

When you approach someone to be your mentor, you might say, "Things aren't going too well for me at home. Sometimes I feel like I just don't have anyone who really listens to me. I was wondering if it would be all right for me to talk to you sometime in person or by phone." If you've chosen the right person, he/she will probably feel honored to be your mentor, because it really is an honor for a caring adult to help a young person in this way. If the person doesn't have the time or seem interested, don't give up. Keep looking until you find someone who can be there for you.

INDEPENDENCE

Maybe your parents are doing an okay job, but you're still having some problems with them. What are all the disagreements about? Usually, they're about the struggle for independence, something that each generation of teens goes through. Now that you're so close to becoming an adult, it may seem as if your parents are trying to hold you back or treat you like a child. Of course, this makes you struggle even harder.

You're growing up fast, and as you near the "finish line" of childhood, you're probably starting to get antsy. Your parents realize that you want to be on your own. And soon you will be. When you reach this point, your parents won't be parenting at such close range anymore (and they know it). They probably figure that they've got only a few more years to make sure that you've really heard and understood everything they've told you since you were little.

As you get older, your parents may continually warn you about every possible danger lurking out there in the world. And their criticisms, reminders, and restrictions may seem never-ending. Does any of this sound familiar:

- "Don't you think you've been on the phone long enough?"
- "Who's ever going to want to live with you if you keep your room like this?"
- "How many times have I told you not to leave dishes in the sink?"
- "When are you going to start your English paper?"
- "Why can't you get a job?"
- "What happened to the money I gave you *last* week?"

These kinds of comments make you feel like a little kid, which is the last thing you need now that you're thinking of yourself as a young adult.

You may even believe that your parents say and do things just to make your life miserable, but this isn't so. Your parents may seem to give you plenty of reasons to believe they don't love you, but remember that there are different ways to show love and caring. Parental love includes concern, protection, and wanting the best for you. Problems surface when you and your parents have a different idea of what's actually "best" for you.

Why can't I pick out my own clothes?

Hey Terra,

I hate the clothes my mom buys for me! She thinks they're so cool, which they aren't, and she thinks it's so great that she got them on sale and saved all this money. What's the point of buying them if there's no way I'd ever wear them?

Embarrassed

Dear Embarrassed,

If you're embarrassed by the clothes your mom buys you, tell her. It might be awkward to be honest with her this way, but how else will she ever know how you really feel?

If you already *have* told her that you don't like the clothes and she still buys them, maybe this is her way of telling you she'd like you to dress differently. Or perhaps she's trying to save money because she can't afford the clothes you really want. If this is the case, would you be willing to earn your own money to buy clothes? Talk to your mom about it and see if there's a way you can make that happen. Another suggestion would be for your mom to give you a monthly clothing allowance equal to what she spends on you already. That way, she wouldn't be spending any more money than she is now, but the difference would be that *you* get to pick out your own wardrobe. In either case, talk to her and see what you can work out together. The important thing is that you understand each other's feelings and treat each other with respect. I hope this helps!

In friendship,
Terra

My parents still treat me like I'm seven, even though I'm seventeen!

Hey Terra,

How do I get my parents to see who I really am? They treat me the same way they did when I was seven. I'm a junior in high school, and I'm a totally different person, but they don't see that. All they see is the picture on top of the TV of a dorky, toothless second-grader who did everything they said.

The Real Me

Dear The Real Me,

Parents who have a hard time letting go need help to see that their teens aren't little children anymore. Once their eyes are opened, they'll adjust their behavior and start relating to you as a young adult. Here are a couple of ideas for helping your parents get to that point:

1. Suggest that your family participate in a parent-teen communication workshop. These are often offered through schools, counseling agencies, community colleges, youth services organizations, and places of worship. This kind of workshop will help you and your parents learn to understand each other better. Once you begin that process, you can work together to improve your relationship.

2. Call a family meeting to work things out. Be patient with and respectful of your parents during the meeting. When it's your turn to talk, explain calmly how their behavior makes you feel. Ask them to change the way they relate to you.

With open communication and continued mature behavior on your part, your parents might start seeing beyond the seven-year-old you once were to the person you have become. Thanks for writing.

In friendship,
Terra

My mom criticizes everything that I do!

Hey Terra,

My relationship with my mom has gotten so bad. Every single thing I do or say bothers her. I get the feeling that she's trying to keep me from growing up or something. Yesterday, she was complaining about my eyebrows, telling me that I look like a "slut" and accusing me of doing stuff that I've never even done with a guy. I can't wait to graduate from high school in a year, get a job, and move out of here.

So Mad

Dear So Mad,

I'm sure your mother wants you to grow up, but it sounds like part of her may not be ready to see you on your own. Maybe she feels sad that your childhood is ending. Instead of telling you how she feels, she's giving you a hard time, which makes you want to get away from her even sooner.

Maybe, on some level, she's contributing to the friction because she thinks that if you two aren't getting along, she won't miss you as much when you leave home. She *is* going to miss you, and you're going to miss her, too. Wouldn't it be nice if you could tell each other the truth and get closer, instead of creating a wall between you?

You'll be on your own soon, so it's important to work on this relationship while you're still living at home. Once you've left, it might be harder for you and your mom to communicate directly. Of course, some parent-child relationships improve after the child moves out, but I suggest that you do your best to work things out before you go.

If you want a peaceful relationship with your mom, stop the blaming and start honestly sharing your feelings. Invite her to go out and do something with you—something the two of you used to enjoy doing together. Get away from your usual "battleground" and have a good time and a good talk.

It's not only up to you to make peace, however. Both people contribute to a deteriorating relationship, and both need to be willing to rebuild. My guess is that your mom wishes as much as you do that you were closer. Why don't you start a conversation with her on that topic? Go for it!

In friendship,
Terra

OPEN COMMUNICATION

Open, honest communication is at the heart of *any* healthy relationship. But this is especially true when it comes to you and your parents. Even though these are the people who helped teach you how to speak, they're often the ones you have the most trouble communicating with!

Who's responsible for the problem? Usually, it's the parents *and* the teen. Open communication flows naturally out of *mutual* trust, respect, and honesty. If the door to good communication is locked, *all* people involved usually hold equal parts of the key that will unlock the door. In other words, the more willing you and your parents are to share your ideas, love, appreciation, praise, objections, and resentments, the more likely you'll be to stay close with each other, now and always.

If communication has shut down between you and your parents, your relationship may feel like all-out warfare with yelling or long, angry silences. Your struggle for independence is natural (even necessary), but it doesn't have to become a battlefield. If you and your parents are arguing often, ask yourself this question: "What are we *really* fighting about?" While the particulars of each fight (curfew, friends, boyfriends/girlfriends, homework) may change, all of them probably boil down to this:

Parent: "I know what's best for you!"
Teen: "No, you don't!"

Do your parents always know what's best for you? No, although they may think they do. Parents don't have all the answers. They may know what *they* would do in a certain situation; they may also remember what they did when they were teens. But you are not your parents, and the times they grew up in were different from now. What was right for them back then may not be right for you, now or ever.

Does this mean your parents' opinions are worthless, and you don't have to listen to them? No. Most parents (even the ones who don't always do the best job) really care about their kids. When people care about you, their ideas are definitely worth listening to. And so are yours.

If you disagree with your parents about something, explain how you feel. Discuss things openly with each other, perhaps during a family meeting. (See pages 234–237 in Chapter 9, "Conflict Resolution Tool Kit," for information about these meetings.) Share your feelings and be open to theirs. Talk and listen to each other with respect.

Having a respectful conversation with your parents may not instantly solve your problems, but open communication is always worthwhile. Besides, the yelling-blaming-crying-silence routine never works, so why not try something that might? When you calmly and thoughtfully discuss all aspects of an issue, your parents are bound to notice a difference. And when they hear you talking in nonblaming ways and listening to them with respect, they might start treating *you* with more respect. Perhaps they'll begin to realize what a trustworthy and mature young adult you are, and that might help you reach agreements that suit your needs and meet their comfort level, too!

My dad is much nicer to my sister than to me

Hey Terra,

My dad is always so sarcastic to me. He makes rude comments about my friends, my clothes, and my hair. I like my hair long, but he says it makes me look like a girl, so there's always that argument. And sometimes I just ask him a question, and he gets mad. Like yesterday, I walked in and said, "Hey, Dad, what's up?" and he said, "Like you *really* care." I was just being friendly, but when he snapped at me like that I just said, "Not really!" and left the room. I felt bad, but I can't talk to him because it always ends up just the same, with us saying mean stuff to each other. He's so much nicer to my sister, and my mom is nicer to me. What should I do?

Feeling Low

Dear Feeling Low,

It sounds like you and your dad are going through a difficult phase. Perhaps your dad has certain ideas of what it means to be a man, and he's critical of you whenever you don't conform to the "manly" ideal he imagines. He's probably not on your sister's case because, in some way, he may see that as your mom's job. Similarly, your mom isn't on your case because she may be leaving that responsibility to your dad.

Here's my suggestion: because you're having an easier time talking to your mom, tell her how you feel about your relationship with your dad. You might say, "Mom, things are really bad between Dad and me. No matter what I do or say, he's on my case. I wish Dad and I could just talk without yelling at each other. Do you think you could ask him not to be so hard on me?" Maybe your mom will try to talk to your dad and make him more aware of how he's contributing to the tension between you two. Then tell your dad that you'd like to talk to him about what's going on. If you'd like, ask your mom to be a part of this conversation, too (not to take sides but to help keep things under control).

If both you and your dad make the effort, you'll likely start communicating better and treating each other with more respect. Remember, though, that it takes work and practice. Good luck!

In friendship,
Terra

Since my dad died, all my mom and I do is fight

Hey Terra,

My dad died last summer, and my life is still a mess. My mom and I used to argue about stuff before his death, but our relationship is lots worse now. She's so awful to me that I don't even want to be home anymore. And the thing is, she acts like she's the only one who's suffering, but I am, too! If she saw my journal she'd know that—not that I'd ever show it to her.

Blue

Dear Blue,

I'm so sorry to hear about your loss. My dad died when I was fifteen, so I understand what a difficult time you're going through. Of course, your mom is grieving, too. You both need time to adjust to this tremendous change in your lives, and your fighting doesn't make it any easier. When you've lost someone important to you, nothing feels right and it's easy to find fault with everything and everyone around you. I'm glad to hear that you keep a journal. Writing is a way to help you sort out these feelings and express what's going on inside.

Another good way to get through this is by talking. I suggest that you talk to your mom about your feelings for your dad, for each other, and for your current situation. This will probably take more than one conversation, but you might start the process by saying, "Mom, ever since Dad died, it seems like all we do is fight. We never talk about him, and it's like we're pretending he was never here. I know you're really sad, and so am I. Maybe you don't want to think about it, but if we could talk about him, maybe we'd both feel a little better."

Your mom needs to understand that she's not the only one who has suffered a loss. You both did. By communicating your feelings, you'll be able to support each other, come to accept your dad's death, and build a stronger bond between you. If it feels like you and your mom can't do this alone, get some help. Find a local grief support group through your place of worship, a hospice organization, or your county's department of social services. You could also use the Internet as a resource. Go to any search engine and look up "grief support."

I wish you and your mom well. Working together, the two of you will have an easier time of it. I hope this helps!

In friendship,
Terra

Teen Age Grief (TAG)
www.smartlink.net/~tag/index.html
Teen Age Grief, Inc. is a nonprofit organization that provides grief support to bereaved teens. This award-winning site was specially created to help teens deal with the death of a loved one.

Teenline
1-800-522-8336
Teenline puts you in touch with trained listeners who care about teens. You can call toll-free any day, from noon to midnight.

I'm afraid to tell my parents that I'm gay

Hey Terra,

I'm sixteen and I'm gay. I tried for a long time to pretend that it wasn't true, but I know it is. From all the reading I've done (and I've done lots!) and talking to other gay teens, I've realized that the best thing for me to do is to accept myself. I believe I have accepted myself, and some of my really good friends, gay and straight, know the truth about me. I'm pretty happy except for the fact that my parents don't know yet.

I've tried to start a conversation with them a few times, but I just don't know what to say. They're pretty cool parents, but I've heard stories from other kids who came out to their parents, thinking it would be accepted, and their parents kicked them out of the house! I don't really believe my parents would do something like that, but I guess there's a part of me that's afraid they might. I can't go on living a lie forever, so what should I do?

Sketch

Dear Sketch,

No one should have to live a lie. You want your parents to know the truth, and that makes sense. Being gay is part of who you are, and your parents need to know that. I understand how scary it is for you to think about telling them. You love them, and you're afraid they might reject you. But telling them is the right thing to do, and you need to take the risk and trust that the love they've always had for you isn't going to disappear.

I can't predict how they'll receive your news, but I suggest that you ask some people you trust for ideas about how to begin this very important conversation. Maybe your gay friends can give you some tips for how to bring this subject up at home, or maybe their parents can tell you what it was like to find out their kid is gay. Your school counselor might also have advice and can point the way toward other resources.

If you're online, you can check out PFLAG (Parents, Families and Friends of Lesbians & Gays), an organization that has chapters in many places around the United States and other countries. Go to: *www.pflag.org.* This site can help you find the words to tell your parents that you're gay and can also prepare you for possible reactions. With support, you can come out to your parents. It's very likely that your parents will come to accept this part of you, but if they need support, too, show them the PFLAG site. I wish you well.

In friendship,
Terra

Be Yourself: Questions and Answers for Gay, Lesbian, and Bisexual Youth
pflag.org/store/resource/BEYOU.html
This site, published by PFLAG (Parents, Families and Friends of Lesbians & Gays) and designed for teens, provides answers to frequently asked questions about homosexuality, stereotypes, health, and coming out.

Parents, Families and Friends of Lesbians & Gays (PFLAG)
www.pflag.org
PFLAG, founded in 1981, has more than 340 chapters nationwide and in 11 other countries. This organization promotes the health and well-being of gay,

lesbian, and bisexual people, their families, and friends. At this site, you'll find support for coming out to friends and family. To find the PFLAG chapter nearest you, go to: *www.pflag.org/chapter.html*.

Trevor Helpline
1-800-850-8078
This hotline provides twenty-four hour telephone counseling for gay youth or anyone who is seeking help or someone to talk to.

My parents don't know what they're talking about

Hey Terra,

My parents constantly make assumptions about what's going on between me and my boyfriend. They say stuff like, "So are you and your boyfriend pretty serious? You're not going steady are you?" It's so embarrassing, and nobody even talks that way anymore! When they ask me these questions, it feels like a total invasion of my privacy. I hate it when they do that, especially since they don't know what they're talking about.

Misunderstood

Dear Misunderstood,

Why is communication so difficult between you and your parents? Perhaps you aren't talking to them about what's going on in your life. Because they can't read your mind, they have to observe you to get any information. It sounds as if they think you and your boyfriend are serious. If they're wrong about this, explain what's really going on. You might start a conversation with them by saying, "It really bothers me when you act like you know what's going on between my boyfriend and me. I realize that I haven't been telling you much; this is partly because I feel like you don't respect my privacy. Could we talk about that?"

Your parents care about you and are concerned about your well-being. Perhaps you could tell them a little about your relationship with your boyfriend, even simple things like where you're going if you're planning a night out and when you'll be back. That kind of information will probably help put their minds at ease and make them willing to give you more privacy. Thanks for writing.

In friendship,
Terra

My dad is a racist

Hey Terra,

I really love my dad, but we totally disagree about being friends with people of color. He really believes that white people are better than other people. I hate to admit it, but he's a racist! When he uses negative words to describe African-Americans, Asians, and Hispanics, it makes me angry and embarrassed at the same time. People shouldn't be judged by their race. How can I get Dad to realize that?

Frustrated

Dear Frustrated,

I'm assuming you've already told your father how his racist statements make you feel. It's important that he knows this, if you haven't told him yet. You might say, "Dad, I feel really uncomfortable when you use certain words to describe people of color. You know the words I'm talking about. It makes me angry and sad that you lump people together and stick nasty labels on them. I'd really appreciate it if you wouldn't use that language in front of me anymore. If you do, I'm going to have to leave the room, because I just don't like hearing that kind of thing." If you say this calmly and directly, you'll be sending your message in a very powerful way. Your dad may not change, but at least you'll have communicated how you feel.

Racial attitudes can be deeply rooted in people's minds. These prejudices are often formed in childhood and can be very difficult to change. But this doesn't mean you can't find other things about your father that you do admire.

I respect you for continuing to choose your friends based on their character and *not* on the color of their skin. You have good values. Stick to them!

In friendship,
Terra

Everything You Need to Know About Racism by Nasoan Sheftel-Gomes (New York: Rosen Publishing Group, 1998). This helpful resource asks: How did racism begin in America? How does it affect you? How can you make a difference? In addition to the answers to these questions, and many more, this book includes a "Where to Go for Help" section, plus practical ways to detect, cope with, and eliminate racism.

I can't get along with my stepdad

Hey Terra,

My dad left when I was little, and I never knew him. My mom remarried about a year ago. My problem is my stepfather—he and I just don't get along. He has opinions about everything, and he acts like he's this really tough dude. And just because he's married to my mom, I've got to listen to him. No way! I never listen to anything he says even though my mom says I should. I feel like "Who does this guy think he is?" He's not my dad so why should he think I'm going to put up with this? I'm not! We fight a lot. He calls me a punk, and that really makes me mad. As soon as I graduate next year (even before I start college), I'm getting so far away from here. Do you have any suggestions about how I can get him off of my back until then?

Outta Here

Dear Outta Here,

This kind of situation sometimes happens between teens and new stepparents. I understand how you might resent someone suddenly coming into your life and trying to tell you what to do and how to be.

It sounds like you and your stepdad are locked into a bad habit of relating to each other mostly in anger. He yells at you, and you resent it so you yell back. Then he probably thinks you're being disrespectful, so he yells some more. Through your behavior, you're both reinforcing the wall between you.

How can you tear down this wall? Start by talking to your mom. Since you two have probably developed your own ways of handling problems over the years, it would be more appropriate for her to discipline you (if necessary). That way, you and your stepdad could focus on getting to know each other, without so much tension.

Even if you're going to be leaving in another year, it makes sense for your family to get along while you're still there. My suggestion is that you talk to your mother privately about the situation. You might say, "I know I've been rude to my stepdad, but I feel like he watches every move I make—like he's waiting to catch me doing something he doesn't like so he can yell at me. He's not my dad, and I want him to stop bossing me around. I know this upsets you, Mom, and I don't like it either, so I was wondering if you could please talk to him about it. I'll try not to be rude to him if he'll back off. Okay?"

I hope your mom can help out. If the discipline stops on your stepdad's part and the rudeness stops on yours, the relationship has a good chance of improving. Then you might actually start to enjoy having a dad again. I wish you well.

In friendship,
Terra

My parents are splitting up, and my mom wants to move!

Hey Terra,

My mom and dad are getting a divorce because my dad fell in love with another woman. If my mom didn't yell at him all the time, maybe he wouldn't have fallen in love with somebody else. Anyway, my mom is moving to this little town to be near my grandparents, and I don't want to go! I feel like she's trying to ruin my life by taking me away from my school and my friends. I tried to tell her this, but she didn't listen. Also, this town is in another state, and if we move there, I won't get to see my dad very much.

I don't think that what my dad did was right, but I love him and he treats me with a lot more respect than my mom does. I think I want to live with him, but I know that would really hurt my mom. What should I do? Help!

Bootsy

Dear Bootsy,

This is a very difficult situation. When parents divorce, it stresses out everyone involved. Your mom is obviously upset and angry, and she's lashing out at your dad. I suggest that you sit down and talk calmly with her about how you're feeling. Doing so might help her understand how much this move will upset you. Although your mom is wrapped up in her own feelings right now, it's very important for her to realize how her decisions will affect you, your school-work, your friendships, and your relationship with your dad.

Do you know another adult you trust enough to talk to? Maybe another relative or a school counselor? It would help release some of your feelings, especially if your mom isn't listening right now. It's also important that you talk to your dad about what's going on. He has rights as a parent, and he might be able to help you figure out your future. Some custody arrangements don't allow one parent to take a child to live in another state, and, depending on the laws where you are, you may be old enough to decide which parent you want to live with.

Obviously, there are many issues to discuss. Some have to do with emotions, while others have to do with practical matters. Tell your mom and dad how you're feeling and let them know that you want to be involved in this very important decision. Good luck!

In friendship,
Terra

WholeFamily Center's "Divorce Page"
www.wholefamily.com/kidteencenter/divorceindex.html
This comprehensive site offers personal stories about young people whose families have gone through divorce, including how they felt at the time and what their lives are like now. The site also includes a Teen Center that features teen advisors who answer questions about adolescent issues and health.

My parents are pressuring me to get all A's

Hey Terra,

I go to a private school, and my parents are stressing me out about how much the tuition costs and what a sacrifice they're making for me. I'm feeling pressured already by the amount of work the teachers give us and worrying about doing well enough to get into a good college. When my parents say stuff like, "B's just aren't good enough" and "You should be getting A's for all the money we're spending," I feel even more stressed. They have lots of money, so I think they might be saying this stuff to make me feel guilty. All I know is that I get a stomachache when they say that kind of stuff to me, which makes it even harder to study!

Help!

Dear Help,

You're absolutely right, it doesn't help anyone perform better when they're being pressured in the way you describe. In fact, the stress of having to live up to other people's standards makes it harder to do your best. But don't assume that the high cost of tuition isn't hard on your parents. Few kids really know what their parents' finances look like. Maybe your parents are feeling money pressures, which makes them doubt whether the high tuition is worth it. They may believe that the only way you're getting a "good enough" education is if you earn all A's.

Explain to your parents that you're doing the best you can (if, in fact, you are trying as hard as you can). The best that you can do doesn't necessarily mean all A's; it just means the best that *you* can do. Not all students, no matter how hard they try, get straight A's. Be open with your parents about the education you're receiving. Make sure they understand the pressure you're under at school but also express to them that you appreciate this opportunity they're giving you. I wish you the best.

In friendship,
Terra

KEEPING AGREEMENTS

To prepare you for adulthood, your parents might be emphasizing the importance of keeping agreements, as well as the consequences for breaking them. These conversations might even lead to huge arguments. Is there anything you can do to convince your parents to loosen up their restrictions? Possibly, if you become a part of the agreement-making process in your family.

Parents think they can make your life easier (that is, less physically dangerous and emotionally painful) if they warn you about the "bad stuff." They advise you and make certain rules in an effort to protect you from harm. Wanting to keep you safe is one way parents show love and caring.

But some parents feel the need to give *lots* of advice. Maybe your parents are this way. Of course, you may not want to hear their recommendations all of the time, but try to understand what might be behind the words. Chances are, your parents are afraid you'll make the same mistakes *they* did. Their warnings and advice are given to prevent history from repeating itself.

Sometimes, when parents are feeling particularly nervous, they might load you down with advice and repeat certain warnings again and again. Maybe they think you're not really listening. And maybe you *aren't* because you resent what they're saying. At times like this, assure your parents (nicely) that you've gotten their message.

Developing and then following a set of agreements is one way to keep a relationship healthy. And when agreements are in place, nobody has to say the same things over and over. If you keep your agreements, and your parents keep theirs, life is much more enjoyable and everyone gets along better.

What should your agreements be? You can probably develop a list that suits your particular family, but if you don't know where to start, begin by thinking about common disagreements between you. Based on the letters I've received over the years, arguments between teens and their parents center around two main categories: *social life* and *schoolwork*. See if some of these exchanges are typical at your home:

Parents: "Be home by 11 P.M. and don't be late!"
You: "Is five minutes after curfew really 'late'?"

Parents: "You've been on the phone too long."
You: "How long is 'too long'?"

Parents: "I expect you to get good grades."
You: "Are B's 'good' enough?"

Parents: "You can't hang out with people who look like that and aren't nice."
You: "Define 'nice.'"

Parents: "You'd better do well in school if you ever want to get into a good college."
You: "What do you consider a 'good' college?"

Parents and teens clearly have different expectations. This is why it's so important to know *exactly* what the agreements are, as well as the consequences for breaking them. Whenever you and your parents make a new agreement, you also need to define the consequences for breaking it. It's often helpful to put a major agreement in writing. Then, when a crisis arises, no important "details" will be forgotten and both you and your parents will be clear on how to deal with the problem.

If you're wondering why you need agreements (and consequences) at all, remember that, as a teenager, you're still a *minor,* and this means you're not yet legally an adult. Until you are, your parents have control over many parts of your life, including where you live and what rules you have to follow. This doesn't mean they have total control over you, though. You have your own life, your own path to travel, and your own choices to make. By working with your parents to create a set of reasonable agreements, you learn to make good decisions, be responsible for your actions, and perhaps avoid making some mistakes. When you do make mistakes, however (and we all do), remember to view them as learning opportunities that can help you grow.

My dad is great about everything except dating

Hey Terra,

I'm fifteen and a half, and my dad has raised me as a single parent for the past six years. I love him a lot, and he's really great except when it comes to dating. He lets me go out with a group of friends on weekends, but he won't let me and my boyfriend be alone together. Also, he makes me come home by eleven o'clock, which is embarrassingly early. I tell him that he can absolutely trust me, and he says he does but he doesn't trust my boyfriend. (How can he not trust him when he's never even met him?) Doesn't all this sound unreasonable for a kid my age? I tell my dad that I can't stand how he's all of a sudden trying to control my life, but he won't listen.

Canary

Dear Canary,

I'm glad you appreciate the wonderful job your dad has done so far. It sounds like you understand that being a single parent is very difficult. Your dad might be having trouble letting you date because it means that you're growing up, which brings a whole new set of emotional challenges for you to experience. Then there are the risks of sex, like pregnancy and sexually transmitted diseases (STDs), which might be why your dad is so concerned about you. Dating also signals that you'll be leaving home soon. Right now, your dad has lots of things to think about, which is why you need to share your feelings with each other. If the two of you can communicate openly, you have a good chance of creating a new, deeper relationship, and maybe your dad won't feel like he's losing you.

When teens start dating, it takes a while for parents to get used to the idea. Work with your dad's comfort level, instead of making demands. For example, you could start with an agreement about your weekend curfew. Your dad doesn't necessarily want you home by eleven because he stops trusting you after that time. I think he just wants to know that you're safe, so he won't worry as much. Maybe you can agree to always tell him where you're going, who you'll be with, how he can reach you, and what time you'll be home. That way, he might agree to let you stay out later.

Also, invite your boyfriend (and any close friends) to meet your dad. He'll appreciate knowing the people you hang out with. And he may come to trust your boyfriend if he has a chance to get to know him.

If your dad agrees to a later curfew, this is a good start. Do your best to keep his trust by sticking to your agreement. After a few months of following the new curfew, you might ask your dad if you can extend it even later. Again, stick to it so he knows he can trust you. If you take small steps, act responsibly with your new freedom, and maintain a healthy relationship with your dad, you'll probably find him becoming more reasonable. Good luck!

In friendship,
Terra

My parents want to send me to boarding school!

Hey Terra,

My parents freaked out when they caught me and my boyfriend kissing goodnight in his car. Now they're acting like he's a rapist, which is totally ridiculous since he's such a sweet guy who would never hurt me. Besides, we've talked about sex and decided that we aren't ready for that. My parents won't listen to me and just keep saying that they don't trust me anymore. I'm not allowed to talk to my boyfriend on the phone, and my parents are talking about sending me to an all-girls boarding school next year! Their attitude is unfair, and it makes me want to go out and do bad stuff since they don't trust me anyway.

Unfairly Accused

Dear Unfairly Accused,

You don't need to be having sex for your parents to think you are. "Sex" is a word that scares parents big-time. They may worry so much about it that they let their imaginations run wild.

It sounds like in this case your parents overreacted, but it's probably because they want to protect you from harmful situations (real or imagined). You, on the other hand, just want the freedom to live your own life, without their interference.

Your parents have tried to bring you back under their "control," but the result is that you want to act out to get back at them. Before the situation gets out of hand, talk to your parents. You might say, "I need to talk to you about something important. The new restrictions you've put on me are making me feel like you don't trust me. My boyfriend and I have a very healthy relationship, and we've decided that we aren't going to have sex. So I don't want you to worry about that. I'd like us to figure out a way that you can feel comfortable letting me have some more independence. I promise that I'll act responsibly." If you speak honestly and listen respectfully to what they have to say, the three of you probably will be able to come up with a solution that works for everyone. I hope this helps!

In friendship,
Terra

My parents won't let me meet my online boyfriend

Hey Terra,

A guy I met online wants to meet me, but my parents say, "No way!" I know what they're thinking, but this guy is really sweet. What can I do to get them to trust me more?

Trustworthy Tess

Dear Trustworthy Tess,

This really isn't about trusting *you*. It's about your parents not trusting the online guy because they don't know him—and you really don't either. Even though this online guy may seem sweet, you need to know that everyone isn't what they pretend to be, especially on the Internet. It's very easy to lie about your age, background, and interests when you're online. The guy you're chatting with may be exactly who he says he is, but there's an equal chance that he's not.

If your parents don't want you to meet him on your own, maybe they'll agree to go with you to meet him in a public place. The arrangement might feel more comfortable to them, but if not, drop the subject for now. If your parents say that you can't meet him, then *don't* meet him. It's not worth taking chances. I wish you well.

In friendship,
Terra

My parents don't have a clue

Hey Terra,

My parents and I have been fighting about a lot of stuff lately like curfew, my friends, and what I'm not allowed to do. Basically, they act like I don't have the right to live my own life. Teens are supposed to rebel—I know that! But my parents act like they don't have a clue about how to raise a teenage son. If they did, they'd give me way more freedom.

Irritated

Dear Irritated,

Let me tell you a secret: your parents are acting like they don't have a clue about raising a teenage son because they probably *don't* have a clue. Parenting isn't something you automatically know; it's something learned "on the job." This makes it very difficult to have all the answers and to make the best parenting decisions all the time.

You're at an advantage because you know the rules that your friends have to follow when it comes to curfew and other issues. But maybe your parents don't usually discuss that kind of stuff with other parents, so they just have to make the rules up as they go along and do what feels right to them. Sometimes they'll make good decisions, but sometimes they may really mess up—and so will you. Everyone makes mistakes, and no one has life all figured out.

This is why it's good to get into the habit of talking to each other openly. By learning to talk about your feelings instead of fighting, you and your parents will have an easier time coming to grips with this new phase in your lives.

Pick a time to talk when you're not upset and your parents aren't busy or tired. In a calm and mature way, explain that you feel like you're ready for more freedom and responsibility. Be very specific about what you're asking for and what you're willing to do in exchange. The bottom line with most parents is that they want their kids to be safe. Keep that in mind, and hopefully you won't be arguing with your parents so much anymore. Thanks for writing.

In friendship,
Terra

I lost my phone privileges because of bad grades

Hey Terra,

Do you think it's fair that I lost my phone privileges for a month just because I got two C pluses and a C on my report card?

Bum Deal

Dear Bum Deal,

It's clear that your parents believe there's some connection between poor grades and too much telephone time. If you want to prove to them that you can balance school and friends, you've got to raise your grades.

My suggestion is that you work really hard to improve your grades in some or all of your subjects. Talk to your teachers to get ideas about how you can do this. Maybe you need to sit toward the front of the classroom so it's easier to pay attention. Perhaps you need help keeping up with your homework and studying for tests. Tell your parents about what you're doing, so they feel reassured that you're giving your schoolwork top priority.

As things get better at school, show your parents the progress you're making. If they're impressed with the improvement, you might be able to renegotiate your phone privileges.

Maybe you can agree to limit the length of time you spend on each call or to use the phone only after your homework is done.

If you truly make an effort to do your best in school, you'll prove to your parents that you're responsible enough to handle your schoolwork and your social life. They'll see that they can trust you to keep your agreements, which may encourage them to give you more freedom in other areas of your life. And one more thing: besides pleasing your parents, working hard in school can bring you a sense of satisfaction and achievement. I wish you well.

In friendship,
Terra

TRUST AND PRIVACY

Your understanding of trust began with the first relationship you ever had, which was with your parents or other caregivers. These are the people who taught you that human beings are trustworthy. How did they do that? By being there for you. From the very beginning, your survival depended on them. They fed you when you were hungry, and you quickly realized that you could count on them for lots of things. As you grew, they learned they could rely on you, too. After so many years of building trust, it can be especially hurtful if it fades during the teen years.

It's safe to say that we all want to be trusted. We want people to be able to count on us and to believe what we say. The way to earn trust—and keep it—is by sticking to the agreements you make with people, especially your parents.

What happens when you don't? You lose some credibility and trustworthiness. If you make an agreement with your parents and break it, for whatever reason, the foundation of confidence they have in you is weakened a little (or a lot, if you've broken a major agreement). Because your parents don't trust you as much as they did before, they may become suspicious of the things you say or do. They may expect that you'll start breaking *all* your agreements. They may even start checking up on you by listening in on your phone conversations, going through your private stuff, reading your journal, or questioning you about every little thing. This isn't healthy for you or for them. If this is happening in your family, you probably feel like you don't have any privacy. Lack of trust and privacy can lead to resentment on both sides.

When a relationship experiences a break in trust, everyone involved suffers. Fortunately, you can work to rebuild trust. Here's what you can do:

• **Take responsibility for what you did.** Acknowledge the part you played in the situation, explain why you made the choice you did, and describe how you'll handle things differently in the future.

• **Apologize.** Saying "I'm sorry" (and meaning it) will help you and your parents feel better.

• **Make amends.** Ask your parents what they'd like you to do to make up for your mistake, and then do it *willingly.*

When you do something untrustworthy, you (and other people) might feel as if you don't deserve to be trusted again—until you prove otherwise, that is. What happens if you make amends, but your parents *still* don't have faith in you? Let them know how their lack of confidence makes you feel. Find out what you can do to earn back their trust—and then do it.

What happens if you've rarely gotten in trouble and your parents don't seem to trust you anyway? A couple of explanations are possible:

- Maybe your parents weren't trustworthy as teens, so they don't expect you to be (even though you are and they want you to be).

- Maybe the stories they read in the papers and hear on the news make your parents fear that you're doing bad things behind their back.

It's difficult to prove to someone that you're trustworthy if you're already being as honest and reliable as you can be! It's also frustrating if you're telling the truth but your parents don't believe you. The best I can suggest is that you continue to listen to your inner voice, do what you know is right, and always keep the lines of communication open. This way, you're staying true to yourself and your own needs.

My parents read my email!

Hey Terra,

I'm an only child, and my parents are totally nosy. I spend a lot of time in chat rooms and have met a ton of really cool people. We email each other all the time, and I caught my parents reading my email. They read my journal, too. I know this because I found it in a different part of my drawer from where I always put it. They even listen in on my phone conversations. They say they're worried about me, but I haven't done anything wrong. I feel like I want to put a lock on my life!

No Privacy

Dear No Privacy,

Your parents seem super protective. I understand that this can be frustrating, especially since you're not doing anything wrong. However, I suggest that you accept that your parents are the worrying kind, which isn't all that unusual when there's only one kid. In families with more than one child, the worrying usually gets spread around and isn't concentrated on one person.

Your interest in chat rooms probably makes your parents anxious. I'm not saying that your Internet friends are untrustworthy, but there *are* weird people who hang out in chat rooms. That's a reality, so it would help to understand that your parents have reason for concern.

On the other hand, you're entitled to some privacy. Talk to your parents. Calmly explain that you're growing up and that you need your privacy. Tell them that they can trust your judgment. Try to ease their worries by letting them know that when you're online you won't give out your last name, home phone number, or home address to the people you chat with. If your parents see that you're being responsible, they may be more likely to start trusting you. I hope this helps!

In friendship,
Terra

My parents don't trust my friends

Hey Terra,

I'm a freshman, and I've made a couple of new friends. These guys both went to different middle schools than I did, so my parents don't know them. Last week, my friends asked me to do stuff with them Saturday night. I really wanted to but only if I could stay out past ten (the curfew I had when I was in eighth grade and still have). My parents said I couldn't go. When I asked them why, they said, "We don't know these kids, and until we do, we aren't going to trust them." I think this is really unfair for them to judge people they don't even know. These guys are cool, and I totally trust them. So why can't my parents trust me to know who's okay and who's not?

Birch Bark

Dear Birch Bark,

I understand that you're excited about spending time with your new friends. It sounds like it might help if your parents could get to know them, too. If they're as trustworthy as you say, your parents might lighten up.

As a ninth-grader, you naturally want more freedom. You need less supervision than you did when you were younger. That doesn't mean your parents are going to feel comfortable tossing all their rules out the window. Parents usually are better about changing old policies when new ones are introduced gradually.

How about calmly sitting down with them and presenting your case? You might say, "Now that I'm in high school, I feel like I'm ready for more responsibility. I'd like to work out a new system where I could stay out later on weekends, in exchange for letting you know where I am and when I'll be home. I'd also be willing to have you meet my new friends and maybe get to know their parents, so you can feel more comfortable about my hanging out with these guys." This way, you're being mature and responsible. If you talk to your parents sincerely, I believe you'll be able to work something out.

By working together, you can create a solution that reflects your desire for more freedom, your willingness to be more responsible, and your parents' need to know that you're safe. Good luck!

In friendship,
Terra

My mom read a letter about my boyfriend

Hey Terra,

My mom read a letter I wrote to my friend, and she found out about me and my boyfriend and some stuff that we've been doing. Now she says I'm grounded, and I have to break up with him because I'm not allowed to have a boyfriend until I'm eighteen (like she was). I'm sixteen now, and I don't want to wait another two years. I knew she didn't want me to date because she's told me a million times, but I love my boyfriend and I don't want to break up with him. And I'm not going to, even though I told her I would. But what if she finds out again?

Hanging Tough

Dear Hanging Tough,

I think it was an invasion of your privacy for your mom to read that letter. At the same time, it was a betrayal of her trust to date someone when she said you couldn't.

I think it would be a bad idea for you to date behind your mom's back. If she finds out, you may be in worse trouble. Besides, sneaking around won't be good for your relationship with your mom or for your relationship with your boyfriend. And someone else will be affected if you sneak around—*you*. Hiding and lying will most likely make you feel stressed out, angry, and frustrated. It isn't worth the pain.

Here's my advice: talk to your mom. You might say, "Mom, I was wrong to start dating without your permission. I'm really sorry. I should have told you when we first went out. I understand about your rules, but I really like my boyfriend and I don't want to break up. I also don't want to sneak around. Maybe if you got to know him, you'd feel better about us going out. Would it be okay if I asked him over so you could meet him?" This may work for you, and it may not. As long as you're under eighteen, you have to live by your mom's rules. The best you can do is try to resolve your problems openly. I hope she can learn to trust you and that you live up to her trust! Thanks for writing.

In friendship,
Terra

Why don't my parents trust me?

Hey Terra,

I'm an honor-roll student, but nothing I do seems to meet my parents' standards because they always think I could have done better. I'm also a very "good" kid who doesn't smoke or do drugs or anything, but they still don't trust me. How come?

Not Good Enough

Dear Not Good Enough,

My suggestion is that you tell your parents how you feel about the pressure they put on you to excel and about the lack of trust they have in you. Be honest and calm when you have this discussion. Ask them why they act this way and give them a chance to respond. By talking with them respectfully and listening to what they have to say, you might get them to see your point of view. If this doesn't work, keep right on making wise choices and being responsible. I know it hurts not to get the acknowledgment you want and deserve from your parents, but realize that you aren't being "good" for them—but because it's right for *you.* I have a lot of respect for the positive choices you're making in your life. Keep it up!

In friendship,
Terra

Bringing Up Parents: The Teenager's Handbook by Alex J. Packer, Ph.D. (Minneapolis: Free Spirit Publishing Inc., 1992). This entertaining yet informative book offers straight talk and specific suggestions on how teens can improve family relationships, resolve conflicts with parents, and help create a healthier home environment.

CHAPTER 7

sooo cute

s i b s

Sibling Relationships

S iblings have a unique relationship. Most likely, you share at least one biological parent and have spent time growing up in the same home. These factors greatly influence the way you relate to each other. Another unusual aspect of this relationship is that it can't ever end—your siblings will always be "family." As an adult, you may choose not to see or speak to your siblings, but you *still* have a relationship.

You and your brothers and sisters probably have ridden the emotional roller coaster known as "Life in This Family." Sometimes you may yell, scream, or ignore each other completely. Other times, you might be such good friends that you forget you're related. And still other times, your relationship may be so strained that you almost wish you were an only child. Occasional conflicts between people who live together are normal and unavoidable. But sometimes, sibling conflicts are so intense that they make life miserable for the whole family. The good news is you can learn to negotiate "cease fires" in the sibling "wars."

COMPETITION

If you've ever seen a litter of puppies pushing and shoving each other to get closer to their mother's milk, you know it's natural to want to make sure that you get your share. But sometimes the competition may get so extreme between you and your siblings that you start comparing every little thing, as if you were keeping score in a never-ending tournament. Maybe this behavior has been going on so long that you're tired of it; perhaps you'd like to change things, but you don't know how to break the competition "habit." Habits are automatic behaviors (you do them without thinking), and understanding the reason behind any behavior is the first step in changing it.

Most sibling competition stems from jealousy, which often carries with it the feeling of "If there's more for that person, there's less for me." Ever since you and your brother/sister became siblings, you've been forced to share things, which may or may not include a bedroom, a bathroom, food, clothing, the phone, the car, the dog, and so on. You may argue a lot over who gets what, but surprisingly, you probably aren't fighting about *stuff* at all (even though it may look that way when you're wrestling over the remote control). Deep down, the confrontation is about *love*.

Maybe this comes as a surprise, but it's true. On some level, you and your siblings have always competed for the love and attention of your parents, or whoever is raising you. And striving to get your fair share of love is what causes all the other kinds of competition. A typical argument between siblings might sound like this: "It's totally unfair the way you always get more (attention, freedom, love, allowance, whatever) than me!" Followed by . . .

"I do not!"
"You do, too!!"
"Do not!!!"
"DO TOO!!!!"

Maybe you'd like to stop arguing and learn how to live with your siblings peacefully. You can begin by forgetting the idea that life is "fair." If fair means "Everybody gets treated equally," then life is definitely *not* fair. In life, everyone gets a different deal. One deal isn't necessarily *better* than the others, just different. Your personality, the personalities of your parents and siblings, and the order in which you were born all influence your deal. For example, the firstborn usually has a different family experience than the youngest child, who has a different one than the middle child, who has an altogether different one from everybody else. Each sibling position in the family includes its own pros and cons, such as:

Firstborns

• **Pro:** They usually get to do things their younger siblings can't, making firstborns feel more privileged, independent, and mature.

• **Pro:** They're trusted to look after younger siblings when the parents can't be there, making firstborns feel good about themselves, as if they can be counted on.

• **Con:** Parents sometimes side with the younger sibling because they think he/she needs protection from the older one.

• **Con:** Firstborns are often blamed when sibling conflicts occur. Parents may say the older sibling should "know better."

Youngest

• **Pro:** The youngest child often gets to do things an older brother/sister wasn't allowed to do at the same age. That's because by the time a second or third child comes along, most parents are a bit more confident and relaxed about their parenting decisions.

• **Pro:** Parents sometimes maintain a special closeness to the "baby" of the family, offering that child more hugs and signs of affection.

• **Con:** Often, older siblings see themselves as higher up in the family "pecking order." This means they may try to boss the youngest child around. The youngest sibling doesn't have anyone younger to give orders to.

• **Con:** Losing the family's baby label can be difficult. The youngest child might feel as if he/she has to try harder at everything (or give up) because family members expect less of the baby.

Middle children

• **Pro:** Many middle children learn to get along with people of all ages. This is because their unique position in the family gives them more experience with people older and younger than themselves.

• **Pro:** Sometimes parents are so focused on the problems and challenges of their oldest or youngest kids that the middle one ends up with more independence.

• **Con:** Firstborn and youngest kids have more years between them, and that often means less competition; they may get along better with each other than either of them does with the middle child. The middle child is closer in age to both the older *and* the younger child, leading to more competition or conflict.

• **Con:** The middle child never really has the chance to be alone in the spotlight because the older sibling was there first, and then came the baby. As a result, the middle child may question his/her importance in the family.

Of course, lots of other factors affect your relationship with your siblings, including:

• **More than three kids:** In families with more than three kids, the oldest and youngest are still there, of course, but the middle child is harder to identify. (Where's the middle in a group of four or six kids?)

• **Large age differences:** Siblings who are five or more years apart in age might not experience the same jealousy and competition as kids one or two years apart. This is because the firstborn was an only child for a long time and had no one to compete with for the parents' attention. When the next child arrived, the first one was already going off to school, giving both children lots of noncompetitive time with the parents. Siblings separated by many years may also be less competitive because they aren't ever at the same stage of development. Their parents are less likely to compare their children's accomplishments and so are the kids themselves.

• **Stepsiblings, half siblings, and adoptions:** These relationships are often characterized by the typical challenges of all sibling relationships—and then some. Blended families face issues of jealousy and competition, too, and it may be harder for the siblings to communicate openly if they don't know each other very well.

Whichever slot you fit into in your family (oldest, youngest, or somewhere in between), remember that nobody gets the best deal and nobody gets the worst. There are pros and cons to *every* position in *every* family.

Even if your relationship with your brother/sister isn't always great, it's important to realize that having a sibling enhances your life. This relationship provides you with great opportunities to learn about yourself and how to get along with someone close to your own age. If you're a guy who's got a sister or if you're a girl who's got a brother, you already know a lot about relating to guys/girls as friends. This is valuable information that will be useful throughout your life.

Although sibling relationships can be difficult (or seemingly impossible) at times, they create a special kind of closeness and understanding that you just can't find anywhere else. After all, you and your siblings are growing up in the same family! Who else in the world can *totally* understand when you're complaining about problems with your parents? And who else is available in the middle of the night or on family vacations when you need someone to talk to? When you consider all the positive aspects of the sibling relationship, it's much easier to forget about the jealousy and competition, and focus on enjoying each other instead.

My sister always gets the guys I like

Hey Terra,

My sister always gets all the guys I like. She's prettier than me, so they usually fall for her. What should I do?

Ugly Duckling

Dear Ugly Duckling,

If guys are falling for your sister, and she's not doing anything to encourage them, there's not a lot she can do about it except tell the guys that she isn't interested. On the other hand, if your sister is deliberately going after guys that she knows you like, she may be trying to prove that she's "better" than you.

Jealousy can really damage a sibling relationship. Maybe your sister is envious of you, which is why she's trying to prove something or hurt you in some way. Perhaps she wants *you* to be jealous of her. See if you and your sister can talk to each other about your feelings. You might start the conversation by saying, "I have a problem, and I was wondering if you could help me with it. I feel annoyed every time a guy I like falls for you. It's not your fault that guys are attracted to you, but I'd like to figure out a way to not feel so much in competition with you." If you come to her asking for help, she may want to work with you to solve this problem. Good luck!

In friendship,
Terra

I'm just not as great as my brother

Hey Terra,

My older brother just graduated at the top of his class. He's also good looking and a great athlete, and he has a terrific personality. So what's my problem? Well, I recently started going to the same school he just graduated from, and everyone there expects me to be like him. I'm interested in sports, but I'm not a jock or anything. And when it comes to girls, I'm kind of shy. I feel like I have to live up to my brother's reputation, and I hate that kind of pressure.

Living in Shadow

Dear Living in Shadow,

You're an individual with your own unique qualities and gifts. I understand that your brother is a tough act to follow, but he's not in the school anymore and people have short memories. You don't have to compete with him—that's all in your head. If you let this idea control you, you might miss out on all of the opportunities your new school has to offer. And people at the school are going to miss finding out about all the special qualities *you* have to offer.

Because your brother is a terrific person, you're lucky to have him in your life. And I'll bet he thinks he's pretty lucky to have you. In fact, if you asked him, he'd probably be glad to give you some tips on how to be more confident with girls. That's the kind of thing older brothers are for! I hope this helps!

In friendship,
Terra

My parents put all the pressure on me because I'm the "good" kid

Hey Terra,

In my family, I'm the "good" kid, and my younger brother is the "screwup." The thing that gets me is that my parents give me the hardest time whenever anything I do isn't perfect. But when it comes to my brother, he can do something really bad and our parents barely even say anything! What's with that?

Good Kid

Dear Good Kid,

The situation you describe is pretty common. Because your brother has taken on the role as the family "screwup," your parents expect him to make mistakes, and it doesn't surprise them when he does. In fact, my guess is that when he *doesn't* screw up (since nobody makes mistakes all the time), your parents don't even notice. As for you, you're in the role of the "good" kid, and when you mess up, it's such a shock that your parents get upset.

Don't be too hard on your brother: he probably wishes he could be more like you. Find ways that the two of you can have a good time together, so you can move beyond seeing him as the family screwup. You could probably learn some positive things from each other, too. For instance, maybe he could teach you about not having to be perfect all the time, and maybe you could teach him about making good choices and having self-esteem. A relationship with a brother can be very special, so I'd say it's definitely worth working on.

As for the way your parents treat you, talk to them about it. Tell them exactly how their behavior makes you feel. You could say, "When I get good grades and win things, you don't seem to notice, and that makes me feel like I have to do 'bad' stuff to get attention. I'd really appreciate it if you'd show me that you're proud of my accomplishments." Your feelings may be news to them. Either way, it's likely to be the start of an interesting conversation. Go for it!

In friendship,
Terra

I'm so unlike my sister!

Hey Terra,

My sister has always had lots of boyfriends, and I think she has kind of a bad reputation. This year, I started high school, and my sister is a junior. Everyone is always assuming that I'm "hot" like my sister. I'm not and, in fact, I'm embarrassed that people think of her as such a slut!

Red

Dear Red,

It's a funny thing: when someone has a sibling with wonderful qualities, people assume the younger brother/sister will also be a great person; when an older sibling has a not-so-wonderful reputation, it's often assumed that the younger sibling will also be "bad." It's totally unfair, but people are sometimes judged by their siblings (at least until their own unique identities become apparent). I understand that you're uncomfortable with your sister's reputation, but you can't change her past (or even her present) behavior. That's something she has to work on herself, although you can offer her advice and support.

I suggest that you concentrate on being yourself at your new school. It won't be long before people get to know the real you, and then they won't base their opinion of you on your sister.

Sometimes people may still come up to you and say embarrassing things about your sister. I realize that you may feel a sense of loyalty to her, but it's not your job to defend her reputation, especially if she's making poor choices. If someone says something negative about her, you could choose not to overreact. You might simply say, "I don't want to talk about my sister." Or you might say, "I don't feel comfortable with you talking about my sister like that. And I'd appreciate it if you'd stop."

If someone asks you about being "hot" like your sister, you can be direct and say, "I just want you to know, in case you didn't notice, that I'm not my sister. Don't make assumptions about me based on what you've heard about her." Thanks for writing.

In friendship,
Terra

COMMUNICATION PROBLEMS

Poor communication is the cause of most relationship problems. For people who don't spend that much time together, communication difficulties aren't all that noticeable. But for siblings living under the same roof, poor communication is *very* apparent. It often results in frequent arguments, something you (and other people) can't help but notice!

It's normal to argue. People have different ideas, opinions, and points of view. That's what makes the world such an interesting place. But these differences of opinion often lead to conflict. In fact, you and your siblings probably have lots of ongoing issues to resolve. Typical arguments between siblings might start with these words:

- "Who said you could wear my clothes?"
- "It's *your* turn to do the dishes tonight, not mine!"
- "How come you always get to stay out later?"
- "Stay away from my boyfriend/girlfriend!"
- "Don't touch my stuff."
- "I'm the runner in this family, and you're not going out for the track team!"

Maybe some of these statements sound familiar, because this is the way you and your siblings relate to each other. If so, you'll probably admit that this way doesn't work very well. Maybe you'd like it if you and your siblings could have a more peaceful relationship, but you've never imagined that it actually could improve. Well, anything can happen! You can work on improving *any* relationship.

Because you and your siblings have been relating to each other in specific ways for so long, you'll have to work hard to make changes. It's going to take a lot of effort to break the long-established patterns of competing, being jealous, arguing, and blaming. Knowing your brother/sister as well as you do, you might even say "Impossible!" But as the saying goes, "*Impossible* just takes a little longer."

Building healthier relationships requires honesty, trust, and respect. If you're ready to "remodel" your relationship with your brother/sister, talk to him/her about it first. Remember, healthy relationships are a two-way street, and it takes effort on both sides to make things work. But if you *are* willing to work at it, you *can* get along better. You may be older or younger than your siblings and totally different in lots of other ways, but you're still entitled to:

- your feelings
- your opinions
- your chance to be heard
- your desire to get what you need

. . . and so is your sibling. For ideas on resolving conflicts, see Chapter 9, "Conflict Resolution Tool Kit," on pages 229–237.

Believe it or not, brothers and sisters are people, too! So treat each other as you like to be treated. Improving your relationship with your siblings will mean a more peaceful family life, now and in the future. Your parents will be happy to see you getting along so well and, years from now, your family reunions will be much more pleasant!

My twin sister is pushing me away

Hey Terra,

My twin sister and I have always been so close, but something's changed, and I feel like she's pushing me away. What can I do about it?

Twinless

Dear Twinless,

Your sister might be going through a phase where she's trying to become more independent from her ever-present twin, which is a natural urge for each of you. Or she might be struggling with a problem that she's unwilling or afraid to talk about.

I suggest that you talk to your sister about what's going on. You could start the conversation by saying, "I've been feeling lonely for you lately. I miss our talks and feeling that you and I always know what's going on with each other. If you just need some time on your own,

I understand. But if there's something bothering you and you want to talk about it, you know I'm always here for you."

If she opens up to you, great! If she's not ready to share her feelings, let her know that whenever she's ready to talk, you're ready to listen. Remember, a sister is forever. I wish you both well.

In friendship,
Terra

My brother has no respect for my privacy

Hey Terra,

My younger brother is a complete pain. I've told him that I don't like it when he annoys me, but nothing stops him. He has no respect for my privacy or anything. He goes through my stuff, borrows it, and messes it up. I feel like beating him up lots of times, but that's not allowed in our family, even though he tries to do it to me. Is there any help for this, or do I have to wait until I'm eighteen and I move out of the house?

Bro

Dear Bro,

Your brother isn't treating you with respect, and you have a right to be upset! You can be proud of yourself for not using violence to communicate your anger to your brother. You don't say how old he is, and that makes a difference in your situation. You can't reason with a two-year-old, but an eight-year-old is a different story. And if he's twelve or thirteen, well, I'd say he's overdue for a serious conversation with you.

The help for this problem is open communication. Tell your brother how you feel about his behavior. You might say, "Look, when I leave my room, it's important to me that I know no one will mess with my stuff. When you take my stuff without asking and wreck it, I get mad. Can you understand that?" Remember that when it's your turn to talk, he needs to listen, and when it's his turn to talk, you need to listen. If you can help him see that he wouldn't like it if you treated him and his stuff the same way that he treats yours, he'll come to understand your point of view.

If the situation doesn't improve after your conversation, talk to a parent and get support in setting limits for your brother. He needs to learn about respecting other people's privacy and property. Good luck!

In friendship,
Terra

My older brother acts like he's my dad!

Hey Terra,

My brother is twelve years older than I am. He's twenty-six, and he just got married. The thing I don't like is that he's always been really bossy. My mom died when I was six, and because our dad worked, my brother was in charge of taking care of me. I guess that's why he just naturally has gotten used to bossing me around like a substitute dad. What he doesn't seem to understand is that I'm fourteen now, and I don't need him to tell me what to do anymore. He doesn't even live in our house, but he's always talking to my dad about what I'm doing. Then my dad starts changing his mind about stuff he already said I could do. My brother's always telling me what I should and shouldn't do. It's like I have two dads, only my brother is the strict one! I hate it! Help!

Too Many Dads

Dear Too Many Dads,

I'm sorry you lost your mom at such an early age. I'm sure that was very difficult for you, your brother, and your dad. Sometimes in situations where one parent is suddenly gone, other family members shift roles to try to deal with the loss.

It sounds like your brother loves you, but I think you're right: he probably has gotten used to looking out for you. He may be concerned that you'll get in trouble now that you're a teen and he's not living at home anymore. But your brother needs to back off and let your dad be your parent.

Sit down with your dad and tell him how you feel about how overprotective your brother is. Also, let your dad know that you want to be able to trust him in the same way that he wants to trust you. This means that when the two of you make an agreement, he needs to keep his word and not suddenly change his mind because he talked to your brother.

It might be a good idea to have a separate talk with your brother, just to remind him that even though he has known you and loved you since you were a baby, you aren't a baby anymore. Thank him for all he's done, but let him know that having one dad watching over you is plenty! I hope this helps!

In friendship,
Terra

My sister has a drug problem

Hey Terra,

My sister has a drug problem. Neither of my parents will admit she does, but I'm really worried about her. What should I do?

Scared

Dear Scared,

If you haven't already spoken to your sister about her problem, do so. Many people who use drugs don't realize how much this hurts their loved ones. You care a lot about your sister, and she needs to know that. You might say, "I love you, and I'm really worried about your drug use. You're putting yourself in danger. I want you to get some help. Would you be willing to do that?"

Lots of organizations offer support to alcohol- and drug-dependent teens and their families. Local branches of these organizations are listed in the Yellow Pages under Drug Abuse and Addiction Information and Treatment Centers. These listings may also provide a number to a toll-free crisis intervention center where you can talk with a counselor about your sister's problem. It's important to remember that, with support, you and your parents can talk with your sister about her drug use—and hopefully she'll choose to accept the help you lovingly offer. If she isn't ready to admit she has a problem, these organizations can help you sort out your feelings regarding this issue. I wish you the best.

In friendship,
Terra

Al-Anon and Alateen
www.Al-Anon-Alateen.org/
This Web site presents information about Al-Anon, a worldwide organization designed to support families and friends of alcoholics, and Alateen (for younger members). You can find out more about the organization, decide if you want to join a group, and locate meetings in your area.

National Council on Alcoholism and Drug Dependence
www.ncadd.org
This site offers clear information about drug and alcohol dependency, plus a questionnaire to help you evaluate whether you or someone you know has a problem with substance abuse. Calling their toll-free number (1-800-622-2255) will automatically connect you with a trained and caring listener—twenty-four hours a day, seven days a week—to help you sort out drug and alcohol issues.

My brother refuses to talk to me

Hey Terra,

My brother is three years younger than I am, and he's got a really nasty temper. If he doesn't get what he wants, he says rude things to me and my mom, and he throws stuff, too. My mom tries not to give in to him, but it's really hard. Sometimes he gets so mad that he just stops talking to everybody. I'd give anything to live in a more peaceful house. What can I do to be on better terms with my brother?

Burned Out

Dear Burned Out,

If someone refuses to talk to you, it's very difficult to have a healthy relationship. It sounds like you, your mother, and your brother would benefit from some family counseling. I suggest talking with your school counselor first. Explain the situation and how you feel about it. The counselor may have ideas you hadn't thought of or can suggest the next step.

If you're concerned about the cost of family counseling, contact your county mental health department, which may offer counseling for free or at a minimal cost. Also, some family therapists in private practice offer sliding-scale fees (which means that clients pay only what they can afford). The important thing is that you reach out for help. Good luck!

In friendship,
Terra

My sister is leaving for college

Send

Hey Terra,

My sister and I are only eighteen months apart, and we've always been like best friends. My problem is that she's leaving for college in two weeks and won't be back until Thanksgiving. I know it's going to be really strange around here without her. I miss her already! Can you help me please?

Soon to Be an Only Child

Dear Soon to Be an Only Child,

It's so nice to hear about two siblings who love each other enough to be best friends! You and your sister are very lucky to have this kind of relationship, which of course makes it even harder to see her leave. You'll miss her, which I understand completely, but it may help to remember that she's ready to move on to the next stage of her life and has to leave home to do so.

At first, it will be strange without her at home. The biggest challenge may be for you and your parents to learn how to relate as a threesome. But this could be a special opportunity for you to get closer to your parents before *you* leave home yourself. After all, for the first year and a half of her life, your sister had your parents all to herself. Now it's your turn!

As for keeping in touch with your sister, everyone loves getting mail, especially people living far from home. So write to your sister often! She may be busier than you are and may not be able to write as often as you can, but don't let that stop you. Telephone rates are less expensive on weekends, so take advantage of that. And if you both have access to email, this is a very fast and convenient way to communicate. No matter what method of communication you choose, let your sister know what's going on in your life, give her lots of details, and make her promise to keep you posted about all the new things that are happening to her.

Remember that you're not really losing her: sisters are forever, so even if you're not living together anymore, you'll always have a bond. Thanks for writing.

In friendship,
Terra

CHAPTER 8

AUTHORITY FIGURES

Dealing with Authority Figures

The dictionary defines "authority" as having the power or right to control, command, or decide. You may feel anxious and nervous around anyone who has the power to make decisions about your life. You most likely don't want to do or say anything to upset the authority figure (AF). On the other hand, you don't want to have to "kiss up" to that person. And it never helps to act out or to be rude.

So, what's the best way to deal with AFs? Ideally, in any healthy relationship, you can relax and be yourself. And communicate openly and honestly. And treat the other person with respect so that you'll be respected in return.

But is it possible to have a healthy relationship with someone who holds the power to impact your future? Yes! You can learn to communicate honestly and negotiate confidently in *all* relationships, including the ones you have with AFs. That means losing any feelings of nervousness or resentment, so you can really talk with the individual behind the title of teacher, boss, coach, or principal. When you learn to communicate with these people one-on-one, with confidence and maturity, you earn their respect and trust. This makes it easier to resolve issues or handle problems that come up.

COPING WITH THE ANXIETY

Many (but certainly not all) teens relate to AFs in one of two ways: either they realize they're nervous and automatically act shy, or they deny their anxiety and automatically act defiant. Neither way is healthy or helpful.

If you're anxious around AFs, you probably feel powerless. And feeling powerless can cause you to get into the habit of always reacting to authority figures in the same way. If you automatically react to someone—whether an AF, a parent, a boyfriend/girlfriend, a friend, or a sibling—you give up your freedom to be yourself at that moment. This makes it nearly impossible to have a healthy, honest relationship.

How do you pick up a habit like this? If you've ever had a negative experience with an AF in the past, you may have decided that it's best not to question authority because it gets you in trouble. As a result, you feel nervous or powerless in the presence of an AF. Or maybe you had the opposite reaction and decided that giving an authority figure a hard time will make him/her back off and leave you alone. As a result, you've learned to act rude or defensive. Once you recognize an automatic behavior, you can work on changing it.

The first step is to make an effort to get to know the authority figures in your life as individuals, not as people you *think* you already know. Take one of your teachers as an example. Maybe you've never even had a conversation with your teacher, and the only interaction you've had is during class. If this is the case, you might see your teacher as someone you have to put up with for a certain amount of time each school day.

What if you were to get to know your teacher on a more personal level? Start to form a stronger relationship with your teacher by simply saying hi in a friendly way when you pass each other in the hallways, or by staying after class to ask a question. If you're still totally nervous about the idea of talking to an AF in a new way, that's normal. You know that he/she has authority over you, and this can translate to a threat to your well-being. Teachers can fail you, coaches can cut you from the team, and bosses can fire you—plus, they're all older than you. It's natural to feel anxious when dealing with these people. So take a few deep breaths before starting a conversation with an AF. If you want, imagine beforehand what you'll say and rehearse the words in your head. Once you start talking for real, you'll start to relax!

Miguel's English teacher hands back his essay with a **B** and this message at the top of the first page: "If you had proofread this, it would have been worth an **A**." Miguel is angry because he thought he'd written a great essay and didn't see why a few spelling errors and typos were a big deal. After class, he accuses his teacher of being an unfair grader and demands the **A** he deserved.

Is this a healthy way to deal with an AF? No. Miguel was angry, but rather than cooling off and thinking through his options, he tried to force his teacher to change his grade. Instead, he could have apologized for turning in sloppy work and asked for a chance to clean up the essay and resubmit it.

Sherelle, a sophomore, has been on the tennis team since she was in eighth grade. Now she's interested in soccer and wants to quit tennis, but she's afraid to tell the tennis coach about her decision. Sherelle is sure the coach, who she's always been close to, will be angry and hurt—and may never speak to her again. Sherelle decides it would be easier to just stick with the tennis team after all.

Does this relationship seem healthy? Not really. Even though Sherelle feels close to her tennis coach, she's afraid to admit that she's interested in trying out for soccer. Sherelle *assumes* that the coach will get mad or stop speaking to her and, as a result, avoids having an important conversation.

Rico's uncle owns a hardware store and keeps saying that he can't wait until Rico turns sixteen, so he can come work at the store after school. Rico loves his uncle but isn't that interested in hardware. One evening, while eating dinner with his aunt and uncle, Rico says: "I really appreciate that you want me to work with you at the store, but I plan to get an internship at a printing company instead. You know how interested I am in printing and design. Maybe I'll even be able to help you with ads for the store someday."

Is this a healthy sign? Yes! Rico knew his aunt and uncle would be disappointed, but he presented his decision positively and trusted they would understand his choice. He was forthright but sensitive to his aunt and uncle's feelings, so they could be more open to *his*.

When you make an effort to be direct and honest with AFs in your life, you're taking these relationships to a new level. You'll probably discover that these people are a lot more helpful and interesting than you ever imagined they were. You may even realize that they can be sources of advice, support, or understanding (see pages 168–169 to find out about *mentors*). And in the process of getting to know *them*, you're giving them the chance to get to know *you*.

My girlfriend's father embarrasses me

Hey Terra,

My girlfriend's father is always embarrassing me. He's an ex-wrestler and still lifts weights. Whenever I go over there to pick up my girlfriend, he always wants to arm wrestle with me or have a push-up contest or something. I hate doing it because I always lose, badly, but I'm too chicken to say no. What should I do?

Weakling

Dear Weakling,

This guy is physically intimidating, but it doesn't seem as if he really wants to hurt you. His behavior may be his way of trying to communicate with you or get to know you better. What do you think would happen if the next time he challenged you to an arm wrestling match you were to just smile and say, "No thanks"? I doubt he'd put you in a headlock! He'd probably kid you a bit and then back off. Then you could start a conversation with him about something he's interested in (besides wrestling!). This will help you relate to each other in a new way—one that's more comfortable for you. Chances are, you'll get to know him better and vice versa.

If he keeps up the rough behavior, it may help to tell your girlfriend how you feel when her dad acts the way he does. She might tell him to treat you like a guest, not a competitor. I hope this helps!

In friendship,
Terra

I'm so afraid of teachers that I say yes to everything

Hey Terra,

Is it possible to be "too" cooperative when it comes to my teachers? My gym teacher always asks me to stay after class and put away the softball equipment, and I always say yes even though it usually makes me have to rush to my next class. I think it would be more fair if she asked other girls to help sometimes. And my English teacher asked me if I'd baby-sit for her daughter on a Saturday afternoon, which I did, but the little girl was really bratty and I didn't want to sit for her anymore. But then, when my teacher asked me again, I said, "Yes, I'd love to." I guess I want people to like me, but I'm just wondering if I even know how to say "No thank you" to people in positions of authority.

Meek

Dear Meek,

It sounds like you may have trouble saying no because you want everyone's approval. People who always do what's expected of them can find themselves feeling very confined, and this often leads to frustration. It's best to seek a balance between doing what others want and doing what *you* want to do.

If you don't like being late for class, be honest with your gym teacher the next time she asks you to put away the softball equipment. You could say, "I'd like to help, but when I do it alone, I'm sometimes late for my next class. Could you ask someone else to give me a hand, so it will go faster?" Your teacher will probably apologize for assuming that you're always available to help her!

If you don't want to baby-sit for your English teacher's daughter again, tell her so. It's up to you whether to admit exactly why you've changed your mind. You might simply say, "I'm sorry. I'd like to help you out, but I'm not available. Maybe you could ask someone else in the class who lives nearby." On the other hand, you could be very honest and direct and say, "The last time I baby-sat for you, your daughter misbehaved and I had a hard time handling the situation. I don't think I'm the right sitter for her. It might be better to try someone else out." My guess is that your teacher will appreciate your honesty and maturity.

In the future, other adults will ask you to do things you may not want to do, and each time, you'll need to take a moment to ask yourself what your next step will be. Maybe you'll want to help out because it's a nice thing to do. Or maybe you won't have the energy, the time, or the interest. Keep telling yourself that it's okay to say no, as long as you say it with sensitivity and respect. I wish you well.

In friendship,
Terra

HANDLING PROBLEMS

If you've got a specific conflict you'd like to resolve with an AF, it's a good idea to first have a plan. This will help you get a clear picture of what you want to say, which will give you confidence and help put you more at ease.

There's no way to know ahead of time how the conversation will turn out, but there are a few things you can do to make things go more smoothly. Start by imagining the best- and worst-case scenarios. It may even help to list the possibilities on a piece of paper. Suppose, for example, that you need to talk to your boss about something you're not happy with at work. What's the worst that could happen? You might:

- feel uncomfortable and embarrassed
- get yelled at
- get on your boss's bad side
- receive a warning about your behavior and performance
- get fired, which means finding a new job without a positive reference from your boss

How do you feel about each possibility? Do you think you can handle each one? Is the worst as bad as you'd thought? Take some time to write about your feelings, perhaps in a journal.

Now that you've imagined the worst, it's time to imagine the best that can happen. If you were to talk to your boss openly and honestly, you might:

- help him/her see what's bothering you, which could lead to a solution
- receive a thank you for your honesty
- earn your boss's admiration and respect
- get a promotion or a raise

Now that you've thought through each possible outcome, do you believe it's worth it to talk to your boss? Do you feel better about having the conversation, knowing that it may lead to positive results? Write about your thoughts and feelings, and ask yourself if envisioning the best-case scenario has given you courage to take action.

Every situation has many possible outcomes. That's the way it is with life—there are many possible paths to take. If you're unsure about what to do, ask yourself, "What's the worst that could happen?" And then take this one step further and ask, "If the worst *did* happen, what would my options be?" In the above example, if you were to get fired for bringing up a problem to your boss, would that really be so bad? Maybe you're better off leaving this boss and job behind. And maybe this would lead you to seek employment elsewhere—perhaps someplace with a better boss and better pay!

Once you've decided to go ahead and talk to the AF, have a practice conversation (also known as a *role-play*). You can act this out by yourself or ask a friend to help. Here's how to do it:

1. Place an empty chair in front of you. If a friend is helping, have him/her sit in the chair.

2. Imagine the authority figure seated in the chair. If a friend is helping, have him/her pretend to be the AF.

3. You go first. Begin talking to the AF. Say anything you want, even the things you'd never say in real life. Make sure you use a wide range of approaches. For example, you might say, "If it pleases your highness, I need an extension on my term paper because the royal magician made one of my research books disappear, and I must find another copy." Have fun with this exercise, because humor often helps to loosen you up and get your ideas flowing.

4. Give the AF a turn to talk. If you're doing this exercise by yourself, get up and sit in the other chair, and then answer as if you were the AF. If a friend is helping, have your friend pretend to be the AF. Make sure your friend uses a wide range of responses—from serious to funny. For example, your friend might say, "Well, this is highly irregular, but if you promise to clean the royal moat, I will grant your request."

5. Switch seats again. Continue practicing until you feel more comfortable. If a friend is helping, keep taking turns talking and listening. You and your friend could also switch roles. Playing the role of the authority figure yourself might help to reduce your anxiety level.

When you feel ready, make an appointment to talk with your AF. Get together at a time that's convenient for both of you and make sure you can talk privately. During the conversation, tell your side of the story directly and respectfully, and be sure to stick to the facts. (For tips on resolving conflicts peacefully, see Chapter 9, "Conflict Resolution Tool Kit," on pages 229–237.) After you've shared your thoughts, listen to what the AF has to say. Be considerate and sensitive, and don't interrupt. Now that you've both had your say, brainstorm solutions. Can you compromise?

While communicating openly and honestly is always a good idea, it doesn't always work. Some people in positions of authority just aren't open-minded or easy to get along with. They may not appreciate having their decisions questioned by someone younger than they are. If you've tried talking face-to-face and this hasn't worked, you may want to write a letter explaining your point of view.

If you decide to write this type of letter, be sure to express yourself in a way that will be taken seriously, while showing respect for the person in authority. Use "I messages" (for more about this, see pages 232–233), such as:

"I am writing to you to formally request an extension on my research paper. I feel that I need some extra time because my grandmother has been sick, and as a result of spending time with her at the hospital after school, I've fallen behind on my research. I understand that you prefer not to grant extensions (as you told me in our conversation), but I would really appreciate it if you would consider my request. I'll do my best to turn my paper in one week past the deadline. Please let me know if this will be acceptable. Thank you."

The nice thing about writing a letter is that it gives you time to carefully choose what to say, without the AF standing there and watching you struggle to find the right words. It also gives the AF time to read the letter and think about the best way to resolve the issue. Just be sure to reread your letter before you give it to the AF—even let it sit for a day and then read it again. You may want to have a parent or another trusted adult read the letter and give you some feedback, too. You can decide whether to make any revisions.

What happens if conversations and letters don't work? Is there any other way to handle problems with authority figures? Yes: question their authority. I don't mean that you should resort to rudeness or defiance. But in some cases, it's perfectly appropriate to go above an authority figure's head. If you and a certain teacher can't see eye to eye, for example, it may be time to get the principal involved. Or if you and your coach can't resolve a particular issue, you may want to ask a parent for help. Some situations are too difficult to handle on your own, and there's nothing wrong with getting help or support.

Although communicating with people in authority can be challenging, you'll feel better about getting your feelings and opinions out in the open. There's satisfaction in knowing that you acted maturely and did what you could to handle a problem or resolve a conflict successfully.

I shot off my mouth to a teacher

Hey Terra,

I'm in seventh grade, and the other day I had to go back to my locker to get a book. The hallway was really crowded, and I dropped my binder in the middle of everything. It opened, and all the papers came out. I tried to pick them up, but kids were stepping on them. Then this really tough eighth-grade teacher yelled at me to get out of the way. I was stressed and yelled back that I was going as fast as I could. She gave me a really dirty look and asked my name and wrote it down! I heard she's in charge of Honor Society. Now I'm worried that I won't get in, even though I get all A's.

Big Mouth

Dear Big Mouth,

Honor Society is partly about good grades, but that's not the whole picture. Students inducted into the Honor Society are "honorable" in the way they deal with other people. That doesn't mean you never make mistakes or say something you regret. But if you *do* make an error, you act honorably by admitting it.

I suggest that you apologize to the teacher you were rude to. Explain that you were stressed out about losing your binder pages and being late for class. Tell her you weren't thinking about what you were saying and that you're sorry for sounding impolite. If you're sincere, I'm sure she'll understand. She might even admire the fact that you tried to make amends. Good luck!

In friendship,
Terra

My boss insults me and everyone else

Hey Terra,

I just got my first job. I love the work, the other people, and the money, but my boss is very rude. He's got a really loud voice, and he insults me and the other workers. I want to tell him how I feel, but I'm afraid of him.

Headache

Dear Headache,

Sorry to hear about your boss trouble! The important thing is not to give up. Avoiding a confrontation with a boss is only a short-term solution for a long-term problem. Besides, it's not acceptable for him to be rude to you or anybody else.

I know you're scared, but I believe that your boss needs to hear what you have to say. Before you talk to him about his behavior, ask him if you're fulfilling all of your job responsibilities. You might say, "I'm really happy here, and I want to make sure I'm doing the best job I can. I'd appreciate it if you'd tell me exactly the way you want this job to be done." If you're carrying out all of your responsibilities in an efficient way but the insults don't stop, it's time for another conversation. This time you might say, "I don't mean to sound disrespectful, but I just wanted to tell you that I don't appreciate being yelled at or insulted. If I'm not fulfilling my duties, please tell me where I need improvement—but tell me politely." I know this won't be easy to say, and you may need some support. Talk to a parent or another trusted adult about the situation and get some advice.

Although your boss is an authority figure, he doesn't have the right to verbally abuse the people who work for him. There's a chance he may fire you for standing up for yourself, and you'll need to ask yourself if this is a risk you're willing to take. If not, I suggest that you spend some time looking for another job, so you can leave on your own terms. You deserve to feel good about the work you do. I wish you luck!

In friendship,
Terra

I don't like the way that my advisor treats me

Hey Terra,

I'm having a problem with my advisor. The thing is, he always calls me by the wrong name, and half the time when I go to see him he's either not there or on the phone. I'm only a freshman, but I'm afraid if this guy doesn't even know me, he'll never be able to write a good college recommendation for me.

Worried

Dear Worried,

A good advisor can be a wonderful help to a student, suggesting courses, colleges, and potential careers. Your advisor sounds very busy, and this could explain why you haven't gotten the attention you want from him. Don't worry about his letter of recommendation at this point, because you have a few more years before you'll be applying to college. Besides, your high-school record is going to speak for itself, though it certainly would be nice to get support from your advisor.

I suggest that you talk to him. You might say, "I feel like I don't matter much to you, or maybe you're getting me mixed up with another kid and that's why you have trouble remembering my name. I'd like to give you a chance to get to know me better, so we can talk." Your advisor will probably appreciate such respectful and direct communication from you. It might even give you two a new start at forming a relationship.

If, after you've talked to him, the situation doesn't improve, speak to a teacher you trust about switching advisors. This isn't unusual, assuming your high school is large enough to have several advisors.

The important thing is that you let your advisor know how you're feeling. He may not be aware of how his behavior is affecting you. If you tell him, you'll give him a chance to treat you with more respect and to do his job better. I wish you the best.

In friendship,
Terra

My coach picks on a kid on our team

Hey Terra,

My soccer coach is always picking on this kid on our team. He obviously doesn't like the kid, and whenever he gets a chance (like every day at practice), he makes the kid run extra laps for no reason at all. It's gotten to be a joke with the other guys, and they tell the kid he should quit soccer and go out for cross-country or some other sport.

Also, the coach hardly ever lets this kid play, and whenever he does, he yells at him during the game and then pulls him out almost immediately. The kid's not that bad of a player, but I'm sure he'd be a lot better if he got to play more. Anyway, I think the coach is treating him unfairly, and I want to tell him so. The kid's kind of wimpy, and he'd probably never stand up for himself. The problem is that I'm afraid the coach is just going to give me laps to run as a punishment for talking to him about the situation.

What's Right?

Dear What's Right,

I admire your values and the fact that you're listening to your inner voice, which is telling you that something isn't right here. The coach's behavior toward this player sounds totally unacceptable. If your teammate is unwilling to defend himself, maybe there's something you can do to make things better. I suggest that you talk to a teacher you trust about this situation. Explain how it makes you feel to see your teammate being treated this way. The teacher may have ideas for making the coach aware of the way he's picking on this player.

If the situation doesn't improve, I suggest you befriend this player—maybe practice extra with him and help him improve his skills. That might change the coach's view of him and make him more willing to include this player in games. It would probably make you both feel better about soccer. You could also advise this kid to try standing up for himself. If he knows he has at least one person's support (yours), he may feel more confident about speaking his mind. Thanks for writing.

In friendship,
Terra

CHAPTER 9

Conflict Resolution Tool Kit

Throughout this book, you've been learning that open communication is one of the keys to healthy relationships. It allows people to feel respected, which in turn makes them more trusting when sharing their thoughts and feelings. Respectful communication is *effective* communication—it helps you express your needs and work toward getting them met.

When people *don't* treat each other with respect, communication becomes much more difficult or breaks down completely. Here's an example: suppose you forget to wear your watch one day, so you ask the stranger standing behind you in line what time it is. The conversation could go like this:

> **You:** "Hey, dork, what time is it?"
> **Stranger:** "None of your business, creep!"
> **You:** "Jerk!"
> **Stranger:** "Loser!"

This exchange could become more heated or get violent. Even if the encounter doesn't go beyond name-calling, both people are left angry or upset.

When people feel attacked, it's natural for them to get defensive or even counterattack. And because it's difficult to think clearly when threatened, each person involved may become more aggressive. On the simplest level, this is how disagreements turn into wars.

Here's an example of a similar conversation, based on more respectful communication:

You: "Excuse me, could you please tell me what time it is?"
Stranger: (glancing at watch) "Sure. It's just past noon."
You: "Thanks."
Stranger: "No problem."

Clearly, this conversation went much better! The encounter was a positive one because both people showed courtesy and respect. Even the simplest exchanges work best when people speak and listen to each other with respect.

Have you noticed that communication between strangers is sometimes easier than between people who know each other well? For example, have you ever revealed things about yourself to people in a support group or a chat room, because you felt more comfortable sharing your feelings with them than with your own family? Many people—adults and teens alike—have trouble sharing their most private thoughts, emotions, and problems with the people closest to them, and it takes time and effort to learn to open up. Lots of people also have a hard time resolving conflicts with those they're close to (family, friends, boyfriends/girlfriends). For whatever reason, it's difficult to talk, and issues that need to be discussed are buried instead. As a result, nothing gets resolved.

You probably handle conflicts differently with the different people in your life, and sometimes it's anything but easy. With your best friend, you might feel as if you can bring up any issue and deal with it right away. With a boyfriend/girlfriend, however, you might feel unsure about whether it's okay to talk about stuff that's private or difficult. And with a parent, you might sometimes think it's impossible to talk about tough issues without being judged. Although it's a challenge to communicate openly with certain people in your life, resolving conflicts peacefully is always worth the effort.

Why is it so important to know how to resolve conflicts successfully? Because they're bound to come up in any relationship. Issues can range from jealousy, to a desire for more independence, to feeling unappreciated, to wanting more privacy, and on and on. But *all* conflicts have one thing in common: they don't go away on their own. In fact, if they aren't handled, they usually worsen.

Unresolved conflicts add strain to relationships, or may even end them. Sometimes the conflicts build until the people involved explode. When this happens, they may not even remember what the original argument was about.

If you really care about the other person and your relationship, it's worth learning to handle conflicts effectively and nonviolently. Once you've discovered how to do this, you can use this skill in *all* your relationships!

RESOLVING CONFLICTS PEACEFULLY

People often experience uncomfortable feelings just because there *is* a conflict. They may be hesitant to talk about what's bothering them, fearing that doing so will jeopardize the relationship. It's important to remember that any relationship worth having needs open communication as a main ingredient. So even though it may be uncomfortable to talk about your feelings, you've got to do it anyway. When you open up and tell another person how you feel, you're making the relationship stronger and healthier. You're also being brave enough to speak the truth, which makes you feel good about yourself and makes you a positive role model for your friends.

Not everyone has trouble opening up when something's bothering them. In fact, they may be quite vocal about their feelings! If you're the kind of person who tends to yell or vent whenever a conflict arises, you can work on keeping your emotions in check and communicating more effectively. This will make it much easier for you (and everyone else involved) to deal with issues that arise.

On pages 232–234 is a plan for handling conflicts and the emotions they stir up. No matter what your style is when it comes to reacting to a conflict, you can use this plan. It's specially designed to work as both a step-by-step guide *and* a problem-solving tool. Here's how it works: you can focus on a specific communication problem and then read through its corresponding conflict-resolution step and try it out. Or, if you prefer, you can read the whole plan from start to finish. Either way, it might be a good idea to share this with the people close to you so you can all get better at resolving conflicts in nonviolent ways.

A conflict—resolution plan

Problem: You're feeling too emotional to talk
about the situation rationally.
How to Handle It: Cool off before trying to
resolve anything (step #1 tells you how).

Step #1: Calm down. It's very difficult to work out a conflict when you're really angry or upset. If you feel less-than-friendly toward the other person, spend some time by yourself *before* saying anything. Cool off, so you'll be able to think more clearly. It may help to do a breathing exercise. Here's how:

- Close your eyes.
- Take several deep breaths, inhaling slowly through your nose
  and exhaling slowly through your mouth.
- Concentrate on your breath as it enters and leaves your body.
- Repeat this exercise for a few minutes or until you feel calmer.

Are you ready to talk now? If not, take some more slow, deep breaths and think about the word "relax." If you're still too upset to talk, go outdoors and do something physical. Take a walk or run, swim, bike, do push-ups—anything that will get your body in motion. Exerting yourself physically redirects your energy in a positive way. If you can't get outside, find a quiet room and spend some time by yourself. Or put on headphones and listen to music. Draw, write, or do whatever else helps you calm down.

Problem: Everybody's yelling.
How to Handle It: Take turns calmly talking
about your feelings (step #2 tells you how).

Step #2: Talk to each other using "I messages" instead of "You messages." Listen to the difference between the sets of statements that follow:

- "You make me so mad."
- "You always do this, and it's so unfair."
- "You are impossible to talk to! You never listen!"

Such statements sound harsh and can make people feel as if they're under attack. Why? Because these *are* verbal attacks! "I messages," on the other hand, don't put the other person on the defensive:

- "I feel upset when you yell at me."
- "I'm concerned about this situation, and I'd like to find a way to work it out."
- "I'd like to make things right between us."

By focusing on "I" and on *feelings*, no one gets blamed or gets defensive. Even when the person talking says something that you believe is untrue, don't cut him/her off. A person's feelings, no matter what they are, are valid and deserve to be heard. As hard at it might be to sit still and keep quiet, remember that everyone in the conversation is entitled to speak without interruptions.

Problem: Nobody's listening.
How to Handle It: Take turns hearing each other's
point of view (step #3 tells you how).

Step #3: Listen effectively. Start by letting the other person speak first and explain what happened from his/her point of view. Listen with an open mind and an open heart. Don't interrupt, question, judge, or plan what you're going to say next. Just listen.

When it's your turn to talk, explain what happened from your point of view. Make sure that the other person listens to you without interrupting, questioning, or judging. If the other person starts to interrupt, you can say something like, "Please let me finish what I'm saying, and then you can have a turn."

Problem: People are blaming others.
How to Handle It: Take responsibility for your
part in the conflict (step #4 tells you how).

Step #4: Ask yourself what role you played. Instead of worrying about who's to "blame," figure out how each person contributed to the conflict. Think about the other person's point of view, and ask him/her to consider yours. To ensure that all involved take responsibility for contributing to the conflict, have each person answer this question out loud: what could I have done differently?

You might want to invite someone else to *mediate* the discussion, or help it go more smoothly and peacefully. This person has to be trustworthy, impartial, and fair (perhaps a counselor, an adult friend, or a peer mediator at school). It never helps if the outside person starts taking sides or expresses his/her own viewpoint: a conflict is complex enough without another person jumping in!

> **Problem:** You're sure the same conflict will occur again.
> **How to Handle It:** Agree to work at keeping the peace
> (step #5 tells you how).

Step #5: Brainstorm peace-keeping solutions. What compromises have been made? Does everyone feel comfortable with the way the conflict has been resolved? How do you plan to handle this problem if it comes up again? Keep talking and take turns offering ideas for handling future conflicts. Have each person answer this question out loud: what could I do the next time something like this comes up? Be as honest as possible. If you'd like, write down these ideas and make sure everyone involved gets a copy.

It takes two (or more) people to make and break a relationship—and also to patch things up. To resolve a conflict, everyone involved needs to cooperate. If you can't get this cooperation no matter how hard you try, the best you can do is to take responsibility for your part in the conflict, apologize, forgive yourself, and *move on*. Use what you've learned from the situation to build healthier relationships in the future.

FAMILY MEETINGS

Sometimes you have conflicts with certain people that cover all-too-familiar territory ("This same old argument again?!")—especially with parents and siblings, which isn't too surprising since you've spent so many years together. When problems don't get resolved as they occur, they may turn into boomerang issues (they just keep coming back). But here's some news for you: you can handle all those recurring arguments in a new way and be done with them for good! How? By holding a family meeting.

Here's how to do it: start by telling your parents, for example, that you'd like to talk to them about curfew (or whatever issue you're in conflict about). This announcement will show them you're serious, and they'll notice the maturity you've demonstrated by initiating a discussion. After everyone involved agrees to the idea, you can follow the step-by-step family-meeting plan below.

A family-meeting plan

Step #1: Schedule the meeting. Pick a time when everyone is calm and in a relatively good mood. In some families, that time might be difficult to find, but be patient, persistent, and specific:

> "Would right after dinner on Thursday be okay?"
> "How about Saturday afternoon at four?"

Keep suggesting times until you can all agree to one. Then mark your calendar and make sure everyone remembers the appointment.

Step #2: Set some rules for the meeting. Many families discover that some of their communication habits don't work well during a family meeting. For example, perhaps you, or others in your family, are used to cutting someone off when he/she is talking, and then contradicting or invalidating what's being said. Those kinds of habits can derail a family meeting before it even gets going.

So, at the beginning of the meeting, it's a good idea to set up some ground rules. Families are free to develop their own rules, but here are some general ones to get you started:

• **Take turns talking.** Your family may even choose to pass an object of some sort—also known as "the talking stick"—to the current speaker, who holds on to it until he/she is finished. In my own family, we use a wooden spoon for this purpose.

• **Listen attentively without interrupting.** This shows respect, an important ingredient in healthy communication.

• **Stick to the topic at hand.** Don't bring up past problems, because this will only make people angry or defensive.

When it's your turn to talk, follow these guidelines:

• **Watch your tone of voice.** Sometimes you might be saying all the correct words (like "I'm sorry"), but your tone of voice is so negative that the message you're sending is, "I'm *not* sorry at all!" Keeping your attitude and tone of voice *positive* will help your family focus on what you're saying and allow you to resolve the conflict successfully—and that should always be the goal.

• **Don't compare your family to other families.** For example, it never helps to talk about what your friends' parents let *them* do. The standard reply almost always goes something like this, "I don't care how late Pete's mother lets him stay out. You're *my* son and you have to go by *my* rules." Or "Good for Alisha! Next time you enter the parent lottery, hopefully you'll be luckier. But for now I guess you're stuck with me!" Parents resent hearing comparisons like this because it sounds as though you believe the other kid has better parents than you do (and that goes for siblings, too).

• **Avoid words like "You always" or "You never."** When you start blaming, accusing, and putting people down, they usually stop listening and start defending themselves. And when people get defensive, they also tend to get sarcastic and angry. This doesn't help resolve the problem—and may even create new ones.

• **Use "I messages."** Say things like, "I feel like it's time for me to be more responsible for my own life." Or "I feel like you don't respect my belongings." When you talk about your feelings, you aren't verbally attacking or blaming, and the people who are listening to you don't have to "fight back." The conversation stays more calm and on track.

When it's their turn to talk:

• **Listen and watch your body language.** Even though you're not talking, you're still communicating—with your body, that is! *Body language* is what you reveal to others through your facial expressions and your pose. Think of what you might be "silently" communicating when your arms and legs are crossed and you're frowning or you're rolling your eyes. The message you're sending is that you're not really open to what the other person is saying. As you listen, really *listen.* Make sure your facial expression conveys that you're willing to hear the other person's side of the story; you can even nod your head to show that you've heard and understood.

• **Reflect back what you've heard.** Put yourself in the place of the other person and try to understand the feelings behind the words. Then use your own words to "play back" what's been said. For example, "What I hear you saying is that you worry about me a lot when I'm out past my curfew." Or "I'm hearing that you like to borrow my stuff because you admire the things I own." If you do this, the other person will know you've really made an effort to hear his/her point of view.

Some families only call family meetings when there's a major issue to discuss. Other families like to hold meetings on a regular basis to "clear the air" and give everyone a chance to speak their mind. And still other families are used to talking during dinner every night, instead of during scheduled meetings. It doesn't really matter how your family gets together to talk—the important thing is to communicate openly and share your feelings, listen to what other people have to say, and work together to solve problems successfully.

P.S.

Creating and maintaining healthy relationships takes work, and often that work is very difficult. But nothing pays off more in terms of what you give and what you get in return.

When most people look back on their lives, they discover that it's not their job title, possessions, or the amount of money in their bank account that matters. You'll probably find that your real treasures are your close friendships and the loving relationships you have with your family members and other people in your life. If these relationships are strong, they'll always provide you with a safe place to talk about your feelings and be treated with honesty and respect. In fact, positive relationships feel like "home" in the best sense of the word—they're the place where you can take off your shoes, relax, and just be yourself.

May all your relationships be healthy ones!

Annie

Annie

INDEX

ABOUT THE AUTHOR

When Annie Fox's first book *People Are Like Lollipops* (Holiday House, 1971) was published, she wasn't even old enough to legally sign the contract. By the time she turned twenty-one, though, she had decided that helping kids was going to be her life's work. After graduating from Cornell University with a degree in Human Development, and completing her Master's in Education, Annie set out to be a teacher.

After a few years, computers changed her life as she began to explore the ways in which technology could be used to empower young people. She and her husband, David, opened the world's first public access microcomputer facility (Marin Computer Center) in 1977, which led Annie to write her best-selling 1982 book, *Armchair BASIC: An Absolute Beginner's Guide to Microcomputers and Programming in BASIC*. From there, she tried her hand at screenwriting, which brought her back to computers as a writer and designer of children's CD-ROMs. In 1996, Annie came up with the idea for Talk City's The InSite, including the "Hey Terra!" advice section. Terra became one of the most popular parts of the site. Its popularity led Annie to write *Can You Relate?*

When she isn't writing, answering Terra letters, or designing Web sites, Annie enjoys hiking, traveling, drawing, painting, yoga, theater, movies, great food, gardening, and, most of all, hanging out with her husband, their two children (Fayette and Ezra), and their dog (Vermont) and cat (Sea Lips).

Other Great Books from Free Spirit

When Nothing Matters Anymore

A Survival Guide for Depressed Teens
by Bev Cobain, R.N.,C.
Written for teens with depression—and those who feel despondent, dejected, or alone—this powerful book offers help, hope, and potentially life-saving facts and advice. Includes true stories from teens who have dealt with depression, survival tips, resources, and more. For ages 13 & up.
$13.95; 176 pp.; softcover; illus.; 6" x 9"

The Right Moves

A Girl's Guide to Getting Fit and Feeling Good
by Tina Schwager, P.T.A., A.T.,C., and Michele Schuerger
The benefits of good nutrition and regular exercise can last a lifetime. This upbeat guide encourages girls to realize their full potential by developing a healthy self-image, eating right, and becoming physically fit. For ages 11 & up.
$14.95; 280 pp.; softcover; illus.; 7" x 9"

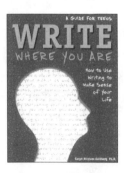

Write Where You Are

How to Use Writing to Make Sense of Your Life
by Caryn Mirriam-Goldberg, Ph.D.
This insightful book helps teens articulate and understand their hopes and fears, lives and possibilities through writing. Not just another writing skills book, it invites teens to make sense of their lives through writing—and shows them how. Recommended for young writers, English teachers, and writing instructors. For ages 12 & up.
$14.95; 168 pp.; softcover; illus.; 7¼" x 9"

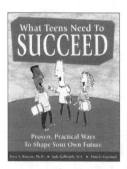

What Teens Need to Succeed

Proven, Practical Ways to Shape Your Own Future
by Peter L. Benson, Ph.D., Judy Galbraith, M.A., and Pamela Espeland
Based on a national survey, this book describes 40 developmental "assets" all teens need to succeed in life, then gives hundreds of suggestions teens can use to build assets at home, at school, in the community, in the congregation, with friends, and with youth organizations. For ages 11 & up.
$14.95; 368 pp.; softcover; illus.; 7¼" x 9¼"

To place an order or to request a free catalog of SELF–HELP FOR KIDS® and SELF–HELP FOR TEENS® materials, please write, call, email, or visit our Web site:

Free Spirit Publishing Inc.
217 Fifth Avenue North • Suite 200 • Minneapolis, MN 55401-1299
toll-free 800.735.7323 • local 612.338.2068 • fax 612.337.5050
help4kids@freespirit.com • www.freespirit.com